SWU-700-011

UNIFORMS OF RUSSIAN ARMY IN THE XVIII CENT. VOL.4

UNDER THE REIGN OF CATHERINE II EMPRESSE OF RUSSIA BETWEEN 1762 AND 1796

From the Viskovatov's greatest work:
"Historical description of the clothing and
arms of the Russian Army"

SOLDIERSHOP PUBLISHING

AUTHOR

Aleksandr Vasilevich Viskovatov born 22 April (4 May New Style) 1804, died 27 February (11 March) 1858 in St. Petersburg, Russian military historian. He graduated from the 1st Cadet Corps and served in the artillery, the hydrographic depot of the Naval Ministry, and then in the Department of Military Educational Institutions. He mainly studied historical artifacts and the histories of military units. Viskovatov's greatest work was the Historical Description of the Clothing and Arms of the Russian Army.

Title: **UNIFORMS OF RUSSIAN ARMY IN THE XVIII Cent. VOL. 4 -**
The Russian Army under the reign of Catherine the Great 1762-1796
By A.V.Viskovatov. Serie edit by Luca S. Cristini. First edition by Soldiershop. September 2016
Cover & Art Design: Luca S. Cristini. Plates re-colorations by Anna Cristini.
ISBN code: 978-88-93272339
Published by Soldiershop publishing, via Padre Davide, 7 - 24050 Zanica (BG) ITALY. www.soldiershop.com

UNIFORMS
OF THE RUSSIAN ARMY IN
THE XVIII Cent.
VOL. 4

UNDER THE REIGN OF CATHERINE II EMPRESS OF
RUSSIA BETWEEN 1762 AND 1796

Catherine II of Russia also known as Catherine the Great 21 April 1729 – 6 November 1796)

HISTORICAL DESCRIPTION OF THE CLOTHING AND ARMS OF THE RUSSIAN ARMY - A.V. VISKOVATOV

Soldiershop is glad to presents the complete collection of the great job made by A.V. Viskovatov dedicated to the uniforms and weapons belonging from the first Zar and Russian emperors to the Russian army during the Napoleonic period, until 1860 about. The time we considered in this volume corresponds to the reigns of Catherine the Great (Catherine II) who reigned since 1762 until his murder on the 6 November 1796.

Our reprint in based on the original 19th century volumes, to be precise the volumes from 4 to 6 are dedicated to the reign of Catherine II; this part is distributed on 3 or 4 volumes.

Our new edition, the first ever published in English, both on paper and digital format, boasts a large number of color plates, many of them unpublished and re-coloured by our team of expert artists and scholars of uniformology. Each volume is based on 100 color plates or more, always accompanied by the original translated text which describes the subjets of the plates.

A unique work in its genre, a must have in any respecting collection!

Aleksandr Vasilevich Viskovatov born 22 April (4 May New Style) 1804, died 27 February (11 March) 1858 in St. Petersburg, Russian military historian. He graduated from the 1st Cadet Corps and served in the artillery, the hydrographic depot of the Naval Ministry, and then in the Department of Military Educational Institutions.

He mainly studied historical artifacts and the histories of military units. Viskovatov's greatest work was the Historical Description of the Clothing and Arms of the Russian Army (Vols. 1-30, St. Petersburg, 1841-62; 2nd ed. Vols. 1-34, St. Petersburg - Novosibirsk - Leningrad, 1899-1948). This work is based on a great quantity of archival documents and contains four thousand colored illustrations.

Viskovatov was the author of Chronicles of the Russian Army (Books 1-20, St. Petersburg, 1834-42) and Chronicles of the Russian Imperial Army (Parts 1-7, St. Petersburg, 1852). He collected valuable material on the history of the Russian navy which went into A Short Overview of Russian Naval Campaigns and General Voyages to the End of the XVII Century (St. Petersburg, 1864; 2nd edition Moscow, 1946). Together with A.I. Mikhailovskii-Danilevskii he helped prepare and create the Military Gallery in the Winter Palace.

He wrote the historical military inscriptions for the walls of the Hall of St. George in the Great Palace of the Kremlin. (From the article in the Soviet Military Encyclopedia.)

CONTENTS

*

MEMOIRS OF THE EMPRESS CATHERINE II
WRITTEN BY HERSELF - PART IV.

FOURTH PART: THE YEAR 1759 (last year of his memoirs)

1759.

On the 1st of January, 1759, the court festivities terminated with a grand display of fireworks between the ball and the supper. As I still kept my room, I did not appear at court. Before the fireworks were let off, Count Peter Schouvaloff took it into his head to present himself at my door, to show me the plan of them before they were let off. Madame Vladislava told him I was asleep, but however she would go and see. It was not true that I was asleep; I was merely in bed, and had my usual little party, which then, as formerly, consisted of Mesdames Narichkine, Siniavine, Ismaïloff, and Count Poniatowsky. The latter, since his recall, had given out that he was ill, but came to visit me, and these ladies loved me sufficiently to prefer my company to the balls and fêtes. Madame Vladislava did not exactly know who was with me, but she was a great deal too shrewd not to suspect that there was some one.

I had told her early that I should go to bed, as I felt weary; and then she did not afterwards disturb me. Upon the arrival of Count Schouvaloff, she came and knocked at my door. I drew the curtain on the side of the screen, and told her to enter. She came in, and brought me the message of Count Peter Schouvaloff, and I ordered her to admit him.

While she went to execute this order, my friends behind the screen were bursting with laughter at the extreme absurdity of the scene—my being about to receive Count Schouvaloff, who would be able to swear that he had found me alone, and in bed, while there was only a curtain which separated my gay little party from this most important personage, who was at that time the oracle of the court, and possessed the confidence of the Empress to a very high degree.

In, therefore, he came, and brought me his plan for the fireworks. He was at the time Grand Master of Artillery.

I began by making apologies for keeping him waiting—only having, I said, just awoke; I rubbed my eyes, saying that I was still quite sleepy. I told a story, not to make Madame Vladislava out a story-teller. After this, I entered into a rather long conversation with him, so much so even, that he appeared anxious to leave, in order not to keep the Empress waiting for the commencement of the fireworks. I then dismissed him. He took his departure, and I again drew aside the curtain. My company, from laughing so heartily, was beginning to feel hungry and thirsty. "Very well," I said, "you shall have something to eat and drink; it is only fair that while you are kind enough to give me your company, you should not die of hunger or thirst." I closed the curtain and rang; Madame Vladislava presented herself.

I told her that I was starving, and desired her to bring me some supper. I said I must have at least six good dishes. When it was ready it was brought to me, and I had it placed by the side of my bed, and told the servant not to wait.

Then my friends from behind the screen came out like so many famished creatures to eat whatever they could find; the fun of the thing increased their appetite. In fact, this evening was one of the merriest I have ever passed in the whole course of my life. When the supper had been devoured, I had the remains cleared away in the same manner as it had been served. I fancy however the servants were a little surprised at my appetite. About the time the court supper had concluded, my party retired also very well pleased with their evening. Count Poniatowsky, when going out, always wore a wig of fair hair and a cloak, and to the question of the sentinels, "Who goes there?" was accustomed to answer that he was a musician to the Grand Duke. This wig made us laugh a good deal that day.

This time my churching, after the six weeks, took place in the Empress' chapel; but no one assisted at it except Alexander Schouvaloff. Towards the end of the Carnival, and when all the fêtes of the city were finished, three weddings took place at court: that of Count Alexander Strogonoff with the Countess Anne Voronzoff, daughter of the Vice-Chancellor, was the first; and, two days after, that of Leon Narichkine with Mademoiselle Zakrefsky; and, on the same day, also, that of Count Boutourline with the Countess Marie Voronzoff. These three young ladies were Maids of Honour to the Empress. At the celebration of these weddings, a bet was made at court between the Hetman Count Rasoumowsky and the Minister of Denmark, Count d'Osten, as to which of the three newly-made husbands should be first cuckolded, and it turned out that those who had bet that it would be Strogonoff, whose bride appeared the plainest of the three, and at the time the most innocent and childlike, won the wager.

The evening preceding the day on which Leon Narichkine and Count Boutourline were married, was an unfortunate one. For a long time, it had been whispered that the credit of the Grand Chancellor was wavering, and that his enemies were getting the upper hand of him. He had lost his friend, General Apraxine. Count Rasoumowsky, the elder, had for a long time supported him; but ever since the influence of the Schouvaloffs had preponderated, he scarcely meddled with anything, except, when occasion offered, to ask for some trifling favour for his friends or connections.

The hatred of Schouvaloff and Voronzoff against the Chancellor was still further increased by the efforts of the Ambassadors of Austria and France, Count Esterhazy, and Marshal de l'Hôpital. The latter thought Count Bestoujeff more disposed for an alliance with England than with France, and the Ambassador of Austria caballed against him, because, while he wished Russia should adhere to her treaty of alliance with the Court of Vienna, and give aid to Maria Theresa, he did not wish that she should take a leading part in a war against the King of Prussia.

The views of Count Bestoujeff were those of a patriot, and he was not easily led; whereas the Messrs. Voronzoff and John Schouvaloff were the tools of the two ambassadors to such an extent that a fortnight before the Grand Chancellor's disgrace, the Marquis de l'Hôpital, Ambassador of France, went to Count Voronzoff, despatch in hand, and said to him, "Monsieur le Comte, here is the despatch of my court, which I have just received, and in which it is said that if, within a fortnight, the Grand Chancellor is not displaced by you, I am to address myself to him, and treat with no one but him."

Then the Vice-Chancellor took fire, and went to John Schouvaloff, and they represented to the Empress that her glory was suffering from the credit which Count Bestoujeff enjoyed throughout Europe. She ordered that a conference should be held that very evening, and that the Grand Chancellor should be summoned to it. The latter sent word that he was ill. This illness was represented as a disobedience, and word was sent to him to come without delay.

He went, and, on his arrival, he was arrested in full conference. He was deprived of his offices, his titles, and his orders, without any one being able to say for what crimes or delinquencies; the first personage of the empire was thus despoiled. He was sent back to his house a prisoner. As all this was pre-arranged, a company of grenadiers of the guard was called out. These, as they passed along the Moïka, where the Counts Alexander and Peter Schouvaloff lived, said to one another, "Thank God, we are going to arrest those cursed Schouvaloffs, who do nothing but invent monopolies." But when the soldiers found that it was Count Bestoujeff whom they had to arrest, they gave evident signs of displeasure, saying, "It is not this man, it is the others, who trample on the people."

Though Count Bestoujeff had been arrested in the very palace of which we occupied a wing, and not very far from our apartments, we heard nothing of it that evening, so careful were they to keep from us all that was going on.

The next day (Sunday) I received, on waking, a note from Leon Narichkine, which the Count Poniatowsky forwarded to me by this channel, which had long since become of very questionable security. It commenced with these words:—"Man is never without resources. I employ this means of informing you, that last night, Count Bestoujeff was arrested and deprived of his offices and dignities, and with him your jeweller Bernardi, Teleguine, and Adadouroff."

I was thunderstruck upon reading these lines, and, having read them, I felt that I must by no means flatter myself that this affair did not affect me more nearly than yet appeared. Now, to make this understood, a few comments are necessary. Bernardi was an Italian jeweller, not without talent, and whose business gave him the entrée to every house. I think that there was scarcely one which did not owe him something, or to which he had not rendered some little service or other, as he went continually to and fro everywhere. He was also intrusted sometimes with commissions from one to the other. A note sent through Bernardi always reached its destination sooner and more safely than if sent by the servants. Now the arrest of Bernardi interested the whole city, since he executed commissions for everybody, and for me among the rest. Teleguine was the former Adjutant of the Master of the Hounds, Count Rasoumowsky, who had had the guardianship of Beketoff. He had remained attached to the house of Rasoumowsky. He had also become the friend of Count Poniatowsky. He was a man of integrity, and one who could be relied on; and when once his affection was gained it was not easily lost. He had always shown a predilection for me, and zeal in my interest.

Adadouroff had been formerly my master in the Russian language, and had remained much attached to me.

It was I who had recommended him to Count Bestoujeff, who, within the last two or three years only, had begun to place confidence in him. Formerly, he did not like him, because he held to the party of the Procurator-General, Prince Nikita Youriewitch Troubetskoy, the enemy of Bestoujeff.

After the perusal of the note, and the reflections which I have just made, a crowd of ideas, one more disagreeable than another, presented themselves to my mind. With the iron in my soul, so to speak, I dressed, and went to mass, where it seemed to me that the greater part of those I saw had faces as long as my own. No one made any remark to me during the day; it was just as if every one was in total ignorance of what had happened. I was silent also.

The Grand Duke, who had never liked Count Bestoujeff, appeared to be rather gay on this occasion, yet behaved without affectation, though he rather kept away from me a good deal. In the evening I was obliged to go to the wedding; I changed my dress, was present at the benediction of the marriages of Count Boutourline and Leon Narichkine, at the ball, and at the supper, during which I approached the Marshal of the wedding, Prince Nikita Troubetskoy, and, under pretence of examining the ribbons of his marshal's baton, I whispered to him, "What do all these fine doings mean? Have you found more crimes than criminals, or more criminals than crimes?" To which he replied—"We have done what we were ordered; but as for crimes, they are still to be discovered. Thus far, the search has not been successful."

Having finished with him, I approached Marshal Boutourline, who said to me—"Bestoujeff is arrested, but we have yet to learn why he is so." Thus spoke the two commissioners appointed by the Empress to investigate the causes that had led to his arrest by Count Alexander Schouvaloff. I also perceived Stambke at the ball, but at a distance, and I saw that his countenance wore an expression of suffering and of despondency. The Empress was not present at either of these two marriages, neither in church nor at the feast. The next day, Stambke came to my apartments, and told me that he had just received a note from Count Bestoujeff, which begged that he would inform me that I need be under no apprehension concerning what I knew; that he had had time to burn everything, and that he would communicate to him (Stambke), by the same channel, the interrogatories which might be put to him.

I asked what that channel was? He told me that it was by a horn-player in the Count's service, who had brought him the note, and that it had been arranged, that for the future, any communications it might be desirable to make should be placed in a particular spot, among some bricks, not far from the Count's house. I told Stambke to take care that this dangerous correspondence was not discovered, though he appeared to be suffering great anxiety himself.

However, he and Count Poniatowsky still continued it. As soon as Stambke had left, I called Madame Vladislava, and told her to go to her brother-in-law, Pougowoschnikoff, and give him the note I was writing to him. It contained only these words:—"You have nothing to fear; there has been time to burn all." This tranquillized him; for, it appears, that ever since the arrest of the High Chancellor, he had been more dead than alive. This it is which occasioned his anxiety, and what the Count Bestoujeff had had time to destroy.

The weak state of the Empress' health, and the convulsive fits to which she was subject, very naturally made all eyes turn to the future. Count Bestoujeff, both from his position and abilities, was certainly not one of the last to do so.

He knew well the antipathy that had long been excited against him in the mind of the Grand Duke. He was also well aware of the feeble capacity of this Prince, born heir to so many crowns. It was only natural that this statesman, like every one else, should wish to maintain himself in his position. For several years past he had seen me laying aside my prejudices against him; perhaps, also, he regarded me personally as the only one upon whom at that time the hopes of the public could rest, in the event of the Empress' death.

These and such like reflections had induced him to form the plan that, on the decease of the Empress, the Grand Duke should be proclaimed Emperor of right, but that at the same time I should be declared a participator with him in the administration; that all existing offices should be continued, and that, for himself, he should receive the lieutenant-colonelcy of the four regiments of guards, and the Presidency of the three Colleges of the Empire, of that of foreign affairs, of War, and of the Admiralty. His pretensions were consequently excessive.

He had forwarded me, through Count Poniatowsky, the draught of this project, written by the hand of Pougowoschnikoff. I had agreed with the former that I should thank him verbally for his good intentions towards me, but that I regarded the plan as difficult of execution. He had had this project written and re-written several times, had altered, amplified, retrenched, and appeared to be quite absorbed by it. To speak the truth, I looked upon it as the effect of mere dotage, and as a bait which the old man was throwing out in order to obtain a firmer hold on my friendship; but I did not catch at this bait, because I regarded it as prejudicial to the Empire, that every quarrel between my husband (who did not love me) and myself should convulse the state; but as the occasion for such a course did not yet exist, I did not wish to oppose an old man who, when once he took a thing into his head, was self-willed and immovable.

This, then, was the project which he had found time to destroy, and concerning which he had sent me word, in order that I might tranquillize those who had been privy to it.

In the mean time, my valet de chambre, Skourine, came to tell me that the captain who guarded Count Bestoujeff was a man who had always been his friend, and who dined with him every Sunday, when he left court and went home.

I said that if this were the case, and if he could be relied on, he should endeavour to sound him, and see if he would allow any communication with the prisoner. This had become the more necessary as Count Bestoujeff had communicated to Stambke, by the mode already mentioned, that he wished Bernardi to be told from him to speak the simple truth when interrogated, and to let him know what were the questions asked. When I perceived that Skourine willingly undertook to discover some means of communicating with Count Bestoujeff, I told him also to try and open some means of communication with Bernardi as well, and see if he could not gain over the sergeant or some soldier who kept guard in his quarter. On the evening of the same day, Skourine told me that Bernardi was guarded by a sergeant of the guards named Kalichkine, with whom he was to have an interview on the morrow; but that having sent to his friend the captain, who was with the Count Bestoujeff, to ask if he could see him, the latter had informed him that if he wished to see him he must come to his house; but that one of his subalterns, whom he also knew, and who was his relation, had cautioned him not to go there, because if he did, the captain would arrest him, and would make a merit of so doing at his expense, and that of this he had boasted to a confidant. Skourine therefore kept away from his pretended friend.

However Kalichkine, whom I had ordered to be gained over in my name, told Bernardi all that was necessary; besides, he was only asked to speak the simple truth, and to this both willingly lent themselves.

At the end of a few days, very early one morning, Stambke came into my room, very pale and greatly frightened, and told me that his correspondence and that of Count Bestoujeff with Count Poniatowsky had been discovered; that the little horn-player had been arrested, and that there was every reason to fear that their last letters had fallen into the hands of Count Bestoujeff's keepers; that he himself expected every moment to be dismissed, if not arrested; and that he had come to tell me this, and to take his leave of me. This information caused me no little anxiety.

However, I consoled him as well as I could, and sent him away, not doubting but that his visit would tend to augment against me, if that were possible, all kinds of ill-feeling, and that I should, perhaps, be shunned as a person suspected by the Government. I was, however, well satisfied in my own mind that I had nothing to reproach myself with against the Government. With the exception of Michel Voronzoff, John Schouvaloff, the two Ambassadors of Austria and France, and those whom these parties made to believe whatever they wished, the general public, every one in St. Petersburg, great and small, was persuaded that Count Bestoujeff was innocent, and that there was neither crime nor delinquency to be laid to his charge. It was known that the day following the evening of his arrest, a manifesto had been concocted in the chamber of Ivan Schouvaloff, which the Sieur Volkoff, formerly first commissary of Count Bestoujeff, and who, in the year 1755, had absconded from his house, and after wandering some time in the woods, had allowed himself to be taken, and who was at this moment first Secretary to the Conference, had to draw up, and which they intended to publish, in order to make known the reasons which had constrained the Empress to act towards the Grand Chancellor in the way she had done. Now, in this secret conference, in which they had to torment their brains to discover offences, they agreed to state that it was for the crime of high treason, and because Bestoujeff had endeavoured to sow dissension between her Imperial Majesty and their Imperial Highnesses; and it was their wish, the very day after his arrest, to banish him to one of his estates, and deprive him of the rest of his property, without trial or judgment.

But there were some who thought that it was going too far to exile a man without crime or trial, and that it was, at least, necessary to look about and see if some crime could not be laid to his charge; and if not, that, in any case, it was indispensable to make the prisoner—who, for some unknown reason, had been shorn of his offices, dignities, and decorations—pass under the judgment of Commissioners. Now, these Commissioners, as I have already stated, were Marshal Boutourline, the Procurator-General Prince Troubetskoy, the General Count Alexander Schouvaloff, and the Sieur Volkoff as Secretary. The first thing these Commissioners did was to give directions, through the department of foreign affairs, to the ambassadors, envoys, and employés of Russia at foreign courts, to send copies of the despatches which Count Bestoujeff had written to them since he had been at the head of affairs.

The object of this was to discover in these despatches some crime or other. It was alleged against him that he wrote just what he pleased, and made statements opposed to the orders and wishes of the Empress; but as her Majesty neither wrote nor signed anything, it was difficult to act against her orders; and, as to verbal orders, she could hardly have given any to the High Chancellor, who for whole years had no occasion to see her; and, as for verbal orders delivered through a third party, they might as easily be misapprehended, as they might be imperfectly delivered, as well as imperfectly received and understood. But nothing came of all this except the order I have mentioned, because none of the employés gave himself the trouble of examining papers ranging over twenty years, and then copying them for the purpose of discovering crimes committed by one whose instructions and orders he himself had followed out, and with whom, therefore, however well meant his efforts, he might become implicated in any faults which might be traced in them. Besides, the mere transmission of these papers would put the crown to a considerable expense; and when, after all, they reached St. Petersburg, there would be enough in them to try the patience of many persons for many years in their attempts to discover and unravel something which, after all, they might contain. The order therefore was never executed; nay, even those who sent it at last grew tired of the business itself, and at the end of a year it was concluded by the publication of the manifesto, which they had begun to compose the day after the Chancellor's arrest.

On the afternoon of the day on which Stambke had come to take leave of me, the Empress sent an order to the Grand Duke to dismiss him, and send him back to Holstein, for that his correspondence with Bestoujeff had been discovered, and that he deserved to be arrested, but that out of consideration for his Imperial Highness, whose minister he was, he should be left at liberty, provided he was immediately sent away. Stambke was immediately sent off, and with

Empress Catherine 2nd visiting Mikhail Lomonosov

his departure ended my interference in the affairs of Holstein. The Grand Duke was given to understand that the Empress was not pleased at my having to meddle with them, and his Imperial Highness was himself inclined that way.

I do not well remember who it was that succeeded Stambke, but I rather think it was a person named Wolff. In the next place, the Empress' ministry formally demanded of the King of Poland, the recall of Count Poniatowsky, as a letter of his, addressed to Count Bestoujeff, had been discovered. It was innocent enough, in fact, but nevertheless was addressed to a so-called prisoner of state. As soon as I heard of the dismissal of Stambke, and the recall of Count Poniatowsky, I prepared myself to expect nothing good, and this is what I did. I summoned my valet de chambre, Skourine, and ordered him to collect and bring to me all my account books, and everything among my effects which could in any way be regarded as a paper. He executed my orders with zeal and exactitude, and when all were brought into my room I dismissed him. As soon as he left the room, I threw all the books into the fire, and when I saw them half-consumed, I recalled Skourine, and said to him, "Look here, and be witness that all my papers and accounts are burnt, in order that if you are ever asked where they are, you may be able to swear that you saw me burn them."

He thanked me for the care I took of him, and told me that a singular alteration had been made in the guard over the prisoners. Since the discovery of Stambke's correspondence with Count Bestoujeff, a stricter watch had been kept upon him, and with this object they had taken from Bernardi the sergeant Kalichkine, and had placed him in the chamber and near the person of the late High Chancellor. When Kalichkine saw this, he asked to have some of the trusty soldiers who were under him when he was on guard at Bernardi's. Here, then, was the most reliable and intelligent man we had introduced into the very apartment of Count Bestoujeff, without having lost all means of communication with Bernardi. In the meantime the interrogatories of the Count were going on. Kalichkine made himself known to him as a man devoted to me, and, in fact, he rendered him a thousand good offices. Like myself, he was convinced that the Chancellor was innocent, and the victim of a powerful cabal—and such, also, was the persuasion of the public.

As for the Grand Duke, I saw that they had frightened him, and had led him to suspect that I was aware of the correspondence of Stambke with the state-prisoner. I perceived that his Royal Highness was almost afraid to speak to me, and avoided entering my apartment, where I remained for the time, quite alone, seeing no one. I would not, in fact, allow any one to come to me, fearing to expose them to some misfortune or inconvenience, and when at court, in order to be avoided, I refrained from approaching any one I thought likely to be compromised by my notice.

On the last days of the Carnival there was to be a Russian play at the court theatre, and Count Poniatowsky begged me to be present, because rumours had been spread that it was intended to send me back to my own country, to prevent my appearance in public, and I know not what besides, and that every time I did not appear at court or at the theatre, every one was anxious to know the reason of my absence, as much perhaps from curiosity as from interest in me.

I knew that the Russian drama was one of the things his Imperial Highness least liked, and even to talk of going there was enough to displease him seriously. On this occasion, too, in addition to his dislike of the national drama, he had another and more personal objection, namely, that it would deprive him of the company of the Countess Elizabeth Voronzoff; as she was in the ante-chamber along with the other maids of honour, it was there that his Imperial Highness enjoyed her conversation or her company at play. If I went to the theatre these ladies were obliged to follow me—a circumstance which annoyed his Imperial Highness, who had then no other resource than to retire to his own apartments to drink. Notwithstanding all this, as I had promised to go to the play, I sent a message to Count Alexander Schouvaloff, desiring him to order a carriage for me, as I intended that day to go to the play. The Count came and told me that my intention of going to the theatre was anything but agreeable to the Grand Duke. I replied that as I formed no part of the society of his Royal Highness, I thought it would be the same to him whether I was alone in my room or in my box at the theatre. He went away, winking his eyes, as he always did whenever anything disturbed him. Some time afterwards, the Grand Duke came into my room. He was in a fearful passion, screaming like an eagle; accusing me of taking pleasure in enraging him, and saying that I had chosen to go to these plays because I knew he disliked them; but I represented to him that he ought not to dislike them. He told me that he would forbid my having a carriage.

I replied that if he did I should go on foot, and that I could not imagine what pleasure he could find in compelling me to die of ennui in my rooms, with no other company but my dog and my parrot. After a long and very angry dispute on both sides, he went away, in a greater rage than ever, and I still persisted in my intention of going to the play.

When it got near the time for starting, I sent to ask Count Schouvaloff if the carriages were ready; he came and told me that the Grand Duke had forbidden any to be provided for me. Then I became really angry, and told him that I would go on foot, and that if he forbade the ladies and gentlemen from attending me I would go alone; and, besides, that I would write and complain to the Empress, both of the Duke and of him. "What will you say to her?" he asked. "I will tell her," I said, "the manner in which I am treated, and that you, in order to secure for the Grand Duke a rendezvous with my maids of honour, encourage him to prevent my going to the theatre, where I might, perhaps, have the pleasure of seeing her Imperial Majesty; and besides this, I will beg of her to send me back to my mother, because I am weary of, and disgusted with, the part I play here: left alone and deserted in my room, hated by the Grand Duke, and not liked by the Empress, I want to be at rest, and a burden to no one; I want to be freed from the necessity of making every one who approaches me unhappy, and particularly my poor servants, of whom so many have been exiled, because I was kind to them, or wished to be so. It is thus that I shall write to her Imperial Majesty, and I will see, moreover, whether you yourself will not be the bearer of my letter." My gentleman got frightened at the determined tone I assumed; he left me, and I sat down to write my letter to the Empress in Russian, making it as pathetic as I could.

I began by thanking her for the kindness and favours with which she had loaded me ever since my arrival in Russia, saying that, unfortunately, the event proved that I did not deserve them, since I had only drawn upon myself the hatred of the Grand Duke and the very marked displeasure of her Imperial Majesty; that as I was unhappy and shut up in my own room, where I was deprived of even the most innocent amusements, I begged her earnestly to put an end to my sufferings, by sending me to my relations in any manner she judged proper; that as for the children, as I never saw them, though living in the same house with them, it made little difference to me whether I was in the same place with them or some hundreds of leagues distant; that I was well aware that she took better care of them than my poor powers would enable me to do; that I ventured to entreat her to continue this care of them; that confident of this, I would pass the rest of my time with my relations, in praying for her, the Grand Duke, my children, and all those who had done me either good or evil; but that my health was reduced by grief to such a state, that I did what I could to preserve my life, at least; and that with this object I addressed myself to her for permission to go to the waters, and thence to my relations.

Having written this letter, I summoned Count Schouvaloff, who, on entering, informed me that the carriages I had ordered were ready. I told him, while handing him my letter for the Empress, that he might inform the gentlemen and ladies who did not wish to accompany me to the theatre, that I would dispense with their attendance.

The Count received my letter, winking his usual wink, but as it was addressed to her Imperial Majesty, he dared not refuse it. He also gave my message to the equerries and ladies, and it was his Imperial Highness who decided who was to go with me, and who was to remain with him. I passed through the ante-chamber, where I found him seated with the Countess Voronzoff, playing at cards in a corner. He rose, and she also, when he saw me—a thing which, on other occasions, he never did. In this ceremony I replied by a low curtsey, and passed on. I went to the theatre, where the Empress did not come on that occasion. I fancy it was my letter which prevented her.

On my return, Count Schouvaloff told me that her Imperial Majesty would have an interview with me herself.

The Count would seem to have informed the Grand Duke of my letter and the reply of the Empress, for, although from that time he never set foot in my room, he used his utmost endeavours to be present at the interview which the Empress was to have with me, and it was considered that this could not well be refused. While waiting for this interview to take place, I kept myself quiet, in my own apartments. I felt persuaded that if the Schouvaloffs had had any idea of sending me home, or of frightening me with the threats of doing so, I had taken the best method of disconcerting the project; for nowhere were they likely to meet with greater resistance to it than in the mind of the Empress herself, who was not at all inclined to strong measures of this kind; besides, she remembered the old misunderstandings in her own family, and certainly would not wish to see them renewed in her time. Against me there could be only one point of complaint, which was, that her worthy nephew did not appear to me the most amiable of men, any more than I appeared to him the most amiable of women; and, as regarded this nephew, her opinions exactly coincided with my own.

She knew him so well that for many years past she could not spend a quarter of an hour in his society without feeling disgust, or anger, or sorrow, and in her chamber, when he happened to be the subject of conversation, she would either melt into tears at the misfortune of having such a successor, or she would be unable to speak of him without exhibiting her contempt, and often applied to him epithets which he but too well merited. I have proofs of this in my hands, having found among her papers two notes written by her own hand, to whom I do not know, though one of them appears to have been for John Schouvaloff, and the other for Count Rasoumowsky, in which she curses her nephew, and wishes him at the devil. In one occurs this expression, "My damned nephew has greatly vexed me;" and in another she says, "My nephew is a fool, the devil take him." Besides, my mind was made up, and I looked upon my being sent away, or not, with a very philosophic eye. In whatever position it should please Providence to place me, I should never be without those resources which talent and determination give to each one according to his natural abilities, and I felt myself possessed of sufficient courage either to mount or descend without being carried away by undue pride on the one hand, or being humbled and dispirited on the other. I knew that I was a human being, and, therefore, of limited powers, and then incapable of perfection, but my intentions had always been pure and good. If from the very beginning I had perceived that to love a husband who was not amiable, nor took any pains to be so, was a thing difficult, if not impossible; yet, at least, I had devoted myself both to him and his interests with all the attachment which a friend, and even a servant, could devote to his friend and master. My counsel to him had always been the very best I could devise for his welfare, and, if he did not choose to follow it, the fault was not mine, but that of his own judgment, which was neither sound nor just. When I came to Russia, and during the first years of our union, had this Prince shown the least disposition to make himself supportable, my heart would have been opened for him, but when I saw that of all possible objects I was the one to whom he showed the least possible attention, precisely because I was his wife, it is not wonderful I should find my position neither agreeable nor to my taste, or that I should consider it irksome, or even painful.

This latter feeling I suppressed more resolutely than any other; the pride and cast of my disposition rendered the idea of being unhappy most repugnant to me. I used to say to myself, happiness and misery depend on ourselves; if you feel unhappy, raise yourself above unhappiness, and so act that your happiness may be independent of all eventualities.

With such a disposition I was born with a great sensibility, and a face, to say the least of it, interesting, and which pleased at first sight, without art or effort. My disposition was naturally so conciliating, that no one ever passed a quarter of an hour in my company without feeling perfectly at ease, and conversing with me as if we had been old acquaintances. Naturally indulgent, I won the confidence of those who had any relations with me, because every one felt that the strictest probity and good-will were the impulses which I most readily obeyed, and, if I may be allowed the expression, I venture to assert, in my own behalf, that I was a true gentleman, whose cast of mind was more male than female, though, for all that, I was anything but masculine, for, joined to the mind and character of a man, I possessed the charms of a very agreeable woman. I trust I shall be pardoned for giving this candid expression of my feelings, instead of seeking to throw around them a veil of false modesty. Besides, this very writing must prove what I have asserted of mind, disposition, and character.

I have just said that I was pleasing, consequently half the road of temptation was already traversed, and it is in the very essence of human nature that, in such cases, the other half should not remain untracked. For to tempt, and to be tempted, are things very nearly allied, and, in spite of the finest maxims of morality impressed upon the mind, whenever feeling has anything to do in the matter, no sooner is it excited than we have already gone vastly farther than we are aware of, and I have yet to learn how it is possible to prevent its being excited. Flight alone is, perhaps, the only remedy; but there are cases and circumstances in which flight becomes impossible, for how is it possible to fly, shun, or turn one's back in the midst of a court? The very attempt would give rise to remarks. Now, if you do not fly, there is nothing, it seems to me, so difficult as to escape from that which is essentially agreeable. All that can be said in opposition to it will appear but a prudery quite out of harmony with the natural instincts of the human heart; besides, no one holds his heart in his hand, tightening or relaxing his grasp of it at pleasure.

But to return to my narrative. The morning after the play, I gave out that I was unwell, and kept my room, waiting patiently for the decision of her Imperial Majesty upon my humble request. However, the first week in Lent I judged it prudent to go to my duty, in order to show my attachment to the Orthodox Church. The second or third week of Lent brought me another bitter affliction. One morning after I had risen, my servants informed me that Count Alexander Schouvaloff had sent for Madame Vladislava. This I thought somewhat strange. I waited her return anxiously, but in vain. About an hour after noon, Count Schouvaloff came to apprise me that her Majesty the Empress had thought fit to remove Madame Vladislava from me. I burst into tears, and said, that of course, her Imperial Majesty had a right to remove or place with me whomsoever she pleased, but that I was grieved to find, more and more, that all who came near me were so many victims devoted to the displeasure of her Imperial Majesty; and that in order that there might be fewer such victims, I begged and entreated him to request her Majesty to send me home to my relations as soon as possible, and thus put an end to a state of things which compelled me to be continually making some one or other miserable.

I also assured him that the removal of Madame Vladislava would not serve to throw any light upon anything whatever, because, neither she nor any one else possessed any confidence. The Count was about to reply, but hearing my sobs, he began to weep with me, and told me that the Empress would herself speak to me on the subject.

I entreated him to hasten the moment, which he promised to do. I then went to my attendants, related what had occurred, and added that if any duenna I happened to dislike took the place of Madame Vladislava, she might make up her mind to receive from me the worst possible treatment, not even excepting blows; and I begged them to repeat this wherever they pleased, so as to deter all who might wish to be placed about me from being in too great haste to accept the charge, for that I was tired of suffering, and as I saw that my mildness and patience had produced no other result than that of making everything connected with me go from bad to worse, I had made up my mind to change my conduct entirely. My people did not fail to repeat all I wished.

The evening of this day, during which I had wept a great deal, walking up and down my room, much agitated both in mind and body, one of my maids, named Catherine Ivanovna Cheregorodskaya, came into my bed-room, where I was quite alone, and said to me very affectionately, and with many tears, "We are all very much afraid you will sink under these afflictions; let me go to-day to my uncle—he is your own confessor as well as the Empress'—I will talk to him, and tell him everything you wish, and I promise you he will speak to the Empress in a manner that will give you satisfaction." Perceiving her good disposition towards me, I told her without reserve the state of matters; what I had written to her Imperial Majesty, and everything else. She went to her uncle, and, having talked the matter over, and disposed him to favour my cause, she returned about eleven o'clock to tell me that her uncle advised me to give out in the course of the night that I was ill, and wanted to confess, and thus send for him, in order that he might be able to repeat to the

Empress what he should hear from my own lips. I very much approved of this idea, and promised to carry it out, and then dismissed her, thanking both herself and uncle for the attachment they displayed for me.

Accordingly, between two and three o'clock in the morning, I rang my bell. One of my women entered. I told her I felt so unwell that I wished to confess. In place of a confessor, Count Alexander Schouvaloff came running to me.

In a weak and broken voice I renewed my request that my confessor should be sent to me. He sent for the doctors, and to these I said that it was spiritual succour I stood in need of; that I was choking. One felt my pulse, and said it was weak; I replied that my soul was in danger, and that my body had no further need of doctors. At length my confessor arrived, and we were left alone. I made him sit by the side of my bed, and we had a conversation of at least an hour and a-half in length. I described to him the state of things past and present; the Grand Duke's conduct to me, and mine towards him; the hatred of the Schouvaloffs, and the constant banishment, or dismissal, of my people, and always of those who had grown most attached to me, and, finally, the hatred of her Imperial Majesty, drawn upon me by the Schouvaloffs; in short, the whole present position of affairs, and what had led me to write to the Empress the letter in which I demanded to be sent home, and I begged him to procure me a speedy reply to my prayer. I found him with the best disposition possible for serving me, and by no means such a fool as he was reported to be. He told me that my letter did and would produce the effect I wished; that I must persist in my demand to be sent home, a demand which most certainly would not be complied with, because such a step could not be justified in the eyes of the public, who had their attention directed towards me. He agreed that I had been treated very cruelly; that the Empress, having chosen me at a very tender age, had abandoned me to the mercy of my enemies; and that she would do far better to banish my rivals, and especially Elizabeth Voronzoff, and keep a check upon her favourites, who had become the blood-suckers of the people, by means of the new monopolies which the Schouvaloffs were every day devising, besides which, they were daily giving the people cause to complain of their injustice, as witness the affair of Count Bestoujeff, of whose innocence the public were persuaded.

He concluded by telling me that he would immediately proceed to the Empress' apartments, where he would wait until she awoke, in order to speak to her on the subject; and that he would then press for the interview which she had promised me, and which ought to be decisive; and that I would do well to keep my bed: he would add, he said, that grief and affliction might cause my death, if some speedy remedy were not applied, and I was not removed, by some means or other, from my present condition where I was left, alone and abandoned by every one. He kept his word, and painted so vividly to the Empress my unfortunate state, that she summoned Count Alexander Schouvaloff, and ordered him to inquire if my condition would allow me to come and speak to her the following evening. Count Schouvaloff came to me with this message, and I told him for such an object I would summon all the strength I had left. Towards evening I rose, and Schouvaloff informed me that, after midnight, he would accompany me to the apartments of her Imperial Majesty. My confessor sent me word by his niece, that everything was going on well, and that the Empress would speak to me that evening. I therefore dressed myself about ten o'clock at night, and lay down fully dressed upon a couch, where I fell asleep. About half-past one, Count Schouvaloff entered the apartment, and told me that the Empress had asked for me. I arose, and followed him. We passed through several ante-chambers, entirely empty, and on arriving at the door of the gallery, I saw the Grand Duke enter by the opposite door, and perceived that he too was about to visit the Empress.

I had never seen him since the day of the play; even when I had given out that my life was in danger, he neither came nor sent to inquire after my health. I afterwards learned that on this very day he had promised Elizabeth Voronzoff to marry her if I happened to die, and that both were rejoicing greatly at my condition.

Having at last reached her Imperial Majesty's room, I there found the Grand Duke. As soon as I perceived the Empress, I threw myself at her feet, and begged her earnestly, and with tears, to send me back to my relations. The Empress wished to raise me, but I remained at her feet; she appeared more grieved than angry, and said to me, with tears in her eyes, "Why do you wish me to send you home? Do you not remember that you have children?" I replied, "My children are in your Majesty's hands, and cannot be better placed, and I trust that you will not abandon them."

She then said to me, "But what excuse should I give to the public in justification of this step?" "Your Imperial Majesty," I replied, "will state, if you think fit, the causes which have brought upon me your Majesty's displeasure, and the hatred of the Grand Duke." "But how will you manage to live when you are with your relatives?" I replied, "As I did before your Majesty did me the honour of bringing me here." To this she answered, "Your mother is a fugitive; she has been compelled to retire, and has gone to Paris." "I am aware of this," I said; "she was thought to be too much attached to the interests of Russia, and the King of Prussia has therefore persecuted her." The Empress again bid me rise, which I did, and she walked away from me to some distance, musing.

The apartment in which we were was long, and had three windows between which stood two tables, containing the gold toilet-service of the Empress. No one was in the room but myself, the Empress, the Grand Duke, and Alexander Schouvaloff. Opposite the Empress were some large screens, in front of which was a couch.

I suspected from the first that John Schouvaloff certainly, and perhaps also his cousin Peter, were behind these. I learnt afterwards that my conjecture was in part correct, and that John Schouvaloff actually was there. I stood by the side of the toilet-table, nearest to the door by which I entered, and noticed in the toilet-basin some letters folded up.

The Empress again approached me, and said, "God is my witness how I wept when you were dangerously ill, just after your arrival in Russia. If I had not liked you, I should not have kept you." This I looked upon as an answer to what I had just said in reference to my having incurred her displeasure. I replied by thanking her Majesty for all the kindness and favour she had shown me then and since, saying that the recollection of them would never be effaced from my memory, and that I should always regard my having incurred her displeasure as the greatest of my misfortunes.

She then drew still nearer to me, and said, "You are dreadfully haughty: do you remember, that at the Summer Palace, I one day approached you, and asked if you had a stiff neck, because I noticed that you hardly bowed to me, and that it was from pride you merely saluted me with a nod." "Gracious heavens! madame," I said, "how could your Majesty possibly suppose that I should be haughty to you? I solemnly declare that it never once occurred to me that this question, asked four years ago, could have reference to any such thing." Upon this she said, "You fancy there is no one so clever as yourself." "If I ever had any such conceit," I replied, "nothing could be better calculated to undeceive me than my present condition and this very conversation, since I see that I have been stupid enough not to understand, till this moment, what you were pleased to say to me four years ago." During my conversation with her Majesty, the Grand Duke was whispering to Count Schouvaloff. She perceived this, and went over to them. They were both standing near the middle of the room. I could not very well hear what they were saying, as they did not speak loud, and the room was large.

At last I heard the Grand Duke raise his voice and say, "She is dreadfully spiteful, and very obstinate." I then perceived they were talking about me, and, addressing the Grand Duke, I observed, "If it is of me you are speaking, I am very glad to have this opportunity of telling you, in the presence of her Imperial Majesty, that I am indeed spiteful to those who advise you to commit injustice, and that I have become obstinate because I see that I have gained nothing by yielding, but your hostility." He immediately retorted, "Your Majesty can see how malicious she is by what she says herself."

But my words made a very different impression on the Empress, who had infinitely more intellect than the Grand Duke. I could plainly see as the conversation progressed, that although she had been recommended, or had herself, perhaps, resolved to treat me with severity, her feelings softened by degrees in spite of herself and her resolutions.

She, however, turned towards him, and said, "Oh, you do not know all she has told me against your advisers, and against Brockdorff, relative to the man you have had arrested." This must naturally have appeared to the Duke a formal treason on my part. He did not know a word of my conversation with the Empress, at the Summer Palace, and he saw his dear Brockdorff, who had become so precious in his eyes, accused to her Majesty, and that by me.

This, therefore, was to put us on worse terms than ever, and perhaps render us irreconcilable, as well as deprive me, for the future, of all share in his confidence. I was thunderstruck when I heard her relating to him, in my presence, what I had told her, and, as I believed, for his own good, and found it thus turned against me like a weapon of destruction.

The Grand Duke, very much astonished at this disclosure, said, "Ah! here is an anecdote quite new to me; it is very interesting, and proves her spitefulness." I thought to myself, "God knows whose spitefulness it proves." From Brockdorff her Majesty passed abruptly to the connection discovered between Stambke and Count Bestoujeff, and said to me, "I leave you to imagine how it is possible to excuse him for having held communication with a state-prisoner."

As my name had not appeared in this affair, I was silent, as if the matter did not concern me. Upon which the Empress approached me, and said, "You meddle with many things which do not concern you. I should not have dared to have done so in the time of the Empress Anne. How, for instance, could you presume to send orders to Marshal Apraxine?" I replied, "I, madame? Never has such an idea entered my head." "What!" she said, "will you deny having written to him? There are your letters in that basin," and she pointed to them as she spoke. "You are forbidden to write." "True," I replied, "I have transgressed in this respect, and I beg your pardon for it; but since my letters are there, these three letters will prove to your Imperial Majesty that I have never sent him any orders; but that in one of them I informed him of what was said of his conduct." Here she interrupted me by saying, "And why did you write this to him?" I replied simply, "Because I took a great interest in the Marshal, whom I like very much. I begged him to follow your orders.

Of the two other letters, one contains only my congratulations on the birth of his son; and in the other I merely presented to him the compliments of the new-year." Upon this she said, "Bestoujeff asserts that there were many others." I replied, "If Bestoujeff says that, he lies." "Very well, then," she said, "since he has told lies concerning you, I will have him put to the torture." She thought by this to frighten me, but I answered that she could, of course, act according to her sovereign pleasure, but that I had never written more than those three letters to Apraxine. She was silent, and appeared to be meditating.

I relate the most salient points of this conversation which have remained in my memory; but it would be impossible for me to recollect all that was said in the course of an interview which lasted an hour and a-half at the least.

The Empress walked to and fro in the apartment, sometimes addressing herself to me, sometimes to her nephew, but more frequently to Count Alexander Schouvaloff, with whom the Grand Duke conversed the greater part of the time, while the Empress was speaking to me. I have already said that I remarked in her Majesty's manner less of anger than of anxiety. As to the Grand Duke, during the whole interview he manifested much bitterness, animosity, and even passion towards me. He endeavoured as much as he could to excite the anger of her Majesty against me, but as he did it so stupidly, and displayed more anger than justice, he failed in his object, and the penetration and sagacity of the Empress disposed her rather to take my part. She listened, with marked attention and a kind of involuntary approval, to my firm and temperate replies to my husband's outrageous statements, from which it was perfectly evident that his object was to clear out my place, in order to establish in it the favourite of the moment.

But this might not be to the Empress' liking, neither might it suit the fancy of the Messrs. Schouvaloff to give themselves Count Voronzoff for a master; but all this transcended the judicial penetration of his Imperial Highness, who always believed in what he wished, and never would listen to anything which appeared the dominant idea of the moment; and on this occasion he dwelt so much upon it that the Empress approached me and said, in a low voice, "I have many other things to say to you, but I do not wish you to be embroiled more than you are already." And with a look and a movement of her head, she intimated that it was on account of the presence of the others that she would not speak.

Perceiving this mark of sincere good-will at so critical a moment, my heart was moved, and I said to her, in a similar tone, "And I also am prevented from speaking, however earnest my desire to open to you my mind and heart." I saw that this made a favourable impression on her. Tears came into her eyes, and to conceal her emotion, and the extent to which she was moved, she dismissed us, observing that it was very late; and, in fact, it was nearly three o'clock in the morning. The Grand Duke went out first, I followed, and just as Alexander Schouvaloff was passing out after me, her Majesty called him back, and he remained with her. The Grand Duke strode on rapidly, as usual, but on this occasion I did not hurry myself to follow him. He entered his apartments, and I mine. I was beginning to undress, in order to go to bed, when I heard some one knocking at the door by which I had entered. On asking who was there, Schouvaloff replied that it was he, and begged me to admit him, which I did. He desired me to dismiss my maids.

They left the room. He then told me that the Empress had called him back, and that, after talking to him for some time, she had charged him to bear to me her compliments, and to tell me not to distress myself, and that she would have another conversation with me quite alone. I made a low bow to the Count, and begged him to present my most humble respects to her Imperial Majesty, and thank her for her kindness, which had restored me to life. I told him that I should look forward to this second interview with the utmost impatience, and entreated him to hasten its time.

He requested me not to speak of it to any one whatever, especially the Grand Duke, who, her Majesty saw, with regret, was greatly irritated against me. This I promised; though I could not help thinking to myself, "But if she regrets his irritation, why increase it by repeating our conversation at the Summer Palace, concerning those people whose society was brutalizing him?"

This unexpected restoration of the favour and confidence of the Empress, gave me, however, great pleasure. The next day I desired my confessor's niece to thank her uncle from me, for the signal service he had rendered me, by procuring for me this interview with her Majesty. On her return she told me that her uncle had heard that the Empress had called her nephew a fool, but said that the Grand Duchess had a great deal of sense. This remark came to me from more quarters than one, as well as that her Majesty, among her intimate associates, was constantly extolling my talents, often adding, "She loves truth and justice; she is a woman of great sense; but my nephew is a fool."

I still continued to keep my room, as before, under the pretext of bad health. I recollect that I read at this time, with the map before me, the first five volumes of the "Histoire des Voyages," and that I was both amused and instructed by the perusal. When tired of these, I turned over the early volumes of the "Encyclopedia," while waiting until it should please her Majesty to admit me to a second interview. I renewed, from time to time, my request to Count Schouvaloff, telling him that I was very anxious to have my destiny decided. As to the Grand Duke, I heard nothing more about him. I only knew that he was impatiently waiting for my dismissal, and that he confidently calculated on afterwards marrying Elizabeth Voronzoff. She came into his apartments, and already did the honours there.

It appeared that her uncle, the Vice-Chancellor, who was a hypocrite, if ever there was one, had become aware of the projects of his brother, perhaps, or rather, it may be, of his nephews, who were then very young, the eldest being only twenty, or thereabouts, and fearing that his newly-revived credit with her Majesty might suffer by it, he intrigued for the commission of dissuading me from demanding my dismissal; for this is what occurred.

One morning, it was announced to me, that the Vice-Chancellor Count Voronzoff requested to speak to me on the part of the Empress. Surprised at this extraordinary deputation, I ordered him to be admitted, though I was not yet dressed. He began by kissing my hand, and pressing it warmly, and then wiped his eyes, from which a few tears fell.

As I was a little prejudiced against him at that time, I did not put much faith in this preamble, by which he intended to show his zeal, but allowed him to go on with what I looked upon as a piece of buffoonery. I begged him to be seated. He was a little out of breath, owing to a species of goitre which troubled him. He sat down by me, and told me that the Empress had charged him to speak to me, and dissuade me from insisting on my dismissal; that her Majesty had even gone so far as to authorize him to beg me, in her name, to renounce a wish to which she never would give her consent, and that for his own part, especially, he conjured me to promise him that I would never speak of it again; adding that the project was a source of great grief to the Empress, and to all good men, among whom, he begged to include himself. I replied that there was nothing I would not willingly do to please her Majesty, and satisfy good men; but that I believed my health and life were endangered by my present mode of existence, and the treatment to which I was exposed; that I made everybody miserable; that all who came near me were either driven into exile or dismissed; that the Grand Duke was embittered against me even to hatred, and that, besides, he had never loved me; that her Imperial Majesty had shown me almost unceasing marks of her displeasure, and that seeing myself a burden to everybody, and nearly worn out with ennui and grief, I had asked to be sent back to my home, in order to free them all from the presence of so troublesome a personage. He spoke to me about my children; I told him I never saw them, and that I had not seen the youngest since my confinement, nor could I see them without an express permission from the Empress, as their apartment was only two rooms distant from her own, and formed part of her suite; that I had not the least doubt she took great care of them, but that being deprived of the pleasure of seeing them, it was a matter of indifference to me whether I was a hundred yards or a hundred leagues away from them. He informed me that the Empress would have a second conversation with me, and that it was greatly to be desired that her Majesty should become reconciled to me.

To this I replied by begging him to accelerate this second interview, and that I for my part would neglect nothing that could tend to realize his wishes. He remained more than an hour with me, and spoke at great length upon a multitude of things. I remarked that the increase of his influence had given him a certain advantage in speech and deportment which he did not formerly possess when I saw him in the crowd; and when discontented with the Empress, with the state of affairs, and with those who possessed her confidence and favour, he said to me one day at court, seeing the Empress speaking for a long time to the Austrian Ambassador, while he and I, and all besides, were kept standing, and tired to death, "What will you wager that she is not talking mere fiddle-faddle to him?" "Good heavens!"

I replied laughing, "what is it you say?" He answered me in Russian, in the characteristic words, "She is by nature...." At length he left me, assuring me of his zeal, and took his leave, again kissing my hand.

For the present, then, I might feel sure of not being sent home, since I was requested not even to speak of it; but I deemed it as well not to quit my room, and to continue there as if I did not expect my fate to be finally decided until the second audience which the Empress was to give. For this I had to wait a long time. I remember that on the 21st of April, 1759, my birth-day, I never went out. The Empress, at her dinner-hour, sent me word by Count Alexander Schouvaloff that she drank to my health. I requested my thanks to be given to her for her kind remembrance of me upon this day of my unhappy birth, which, I added, I would curse, were it not also the day of my baptism.

When the Grand Duke learned that the Empress had sent this message to me, he took it into his head to do the same. When his message was announced to me, I rose, and with a low courtesy expressed my thanks.

After the fêtes in honour of my birth-day, and of the Empress' coronation day, which occurred within four days of each other, I still remained in my chamber, and never went out until Count Poniatowsky sent me word that the French Ambassador, the Marquis de l'Hôpital, had been eulogizing the firmness of my conduct, and observed that the resolution I maintained of never leaving my room could not but be productive of advantage to me.

Taking this speech as the treacherous praise of an enemy, I determined to do exactly the contrary to what he advised; and, one Sunday, when it was least expected, I dressed, and came out of my private room.

The moment I entered the apartment occupied by the ladies and gentlemen in waiting, I remarked their astonishment at seeing me. Some minutes after my appearance, the Grand Duke also entered. He looked equally astonished, and, while I was conversing with the company, he joined in the conversation, and addressed some remarks to me, to which I civilly replied.

About this time, Prince Charles of Saxony paid a second visit to St. Petersburg. The Grand Duke had treated him cavalierly enough on the first occasion, but this time his Imperial Highness thought himself justified in observing no terms with him, and for this reason: It was no secret in the Russian army that in the battle of Zorndorf Prince Charles had been one of the first to fly; and it was even asserted that he had fled without once stopping until he reached Landsberg. Now his Imperial Highness having heard this, resolved that, as a proved coward, he would not speak to him, nor have anything to do with him. There was every reason to believe that the Princess of Courland, daughter of Biren, did not a little contribute to this; for it had already begun to be whispered that there was an intention of making Prince Charles Duke of Courland. The father of the Princess of Courland was constantly retained at Yaroslav. She communicated her hostility to the Grand Duke, over whom she had always contrived to retain a kind of ascendancy. She was then engaged for the third time to Baron Alexander Tcherkassoff, to whom she was married the winter following.

At last, a few days before our going into the country, Count Alexander Schouvaloff came to inform me, on the part of the Empress, that I was to ask this afternoon, through him, permission to visit my children, and that then, upon my leaving them, I should have that second audience with her Majesty which had been so long promised. I did as I was directed, and, in presence of a number of people, I begged Count Schouvaloff to ask her Majesty's permission for me to see my children. He went away, and on his return told me that I could see them at three o'clock.

I was punctual to the time, and remained with my children until Count Schouvaloff came to tell me that her Imperial Majesty could be seen. I went to her, and found her quite alone, and this time there were no screens in the room, and consequently we were able to speak freely. I began by thanking her for the audience she gave me, saying that her gracious promise of it had restored me to life. Upon which she said, "I expect you to reply with sincerity to all the questions that I may put to you." I assured her that she should hear nothing but the strict truth from me, and that there was nothing I desired more than to open my heart to her without reserve. Then she again asked if there really had been no more than three letters written to Apraxine. I solemnly assured her, and with perfect truth, that such was the fact. Then she asked me for details concerning the Grand Duke's mode of life....

(end of Catherine's memoirs)

COMPLETE BIOGRAPHY

Catherine II of Russia also known as Catherine the Great (21 April) 1729 – 17 November 1796), was the most renowned and the longest-ruling female leader of Russia, reigning from 1762 until her death in 1796 at the age of 67. Born in Stettin, Pomerania, Prussia as Sophie Friederike Auguste von Anhalt-Zerbst-Dornburg, she came to power following a coup d'état when her husband, Peter III, was assassinated. Russia was revitalised under her reign, growing larger and stronger than ever and becoming recognised as one of the great powers of Europe.

In both her accession to power and in rule of her empire, Catherine often relied on her noble favourites, most notably Grigory Orlov and Grigory Potemkin. Assisted by highly successful generals such as Alexander Suvorov and Pyotr Rumyantsev, and admirals such as Fyodor Ushakov, she governed at a time when the Russian Empire was expanding rapidly by conquest and diplomacy. In the south, the Crimean Khanate was crushed following victories over the Ottoman Empire in the Russo-Turkish wars, and Russia colonised the vast territories of Novorossiya along the coasts of the Black and Azov Seas. In the west, the Polish–Lithuanian Commonwealth, ruled by Catherine's former lover, king Stanisław August Poniatowski, was eventually partitioned, with the Russian Empire gaining the largest share. In the east, Russia started to colonise Alaska, establishing Russian America.

Catherine reformed the administration of Russian guberniyas, and many new cities and towns were founded on her orders. An admirer of Peter the Great, Catherine continued to modernise Russia along Western European lines. However, military conscription and economy continued to depend on serfdom, and the increasing demands of the state and private landowners led to increased levels of reliance on serfs. This was one of the chief reasons behind several rebellions, including the large-scale Pugachev's Rebellion of cossacks and peasants.

The period of Catherine the Great's rule, the Catherinian Era, is often considered the Golden Age of the Russian Empire and the Russian nobility. The Manifesto on Freedom of the Nobility, issued during the short reign of Peter III and confirmed by Catherine, freed Russian nobles from compulsory military or state service. Construction of many mansions of the nobility, in the classical style endorsed by the Empress, changed the face of the country. She enthusiastically supported the ideals of The Enlightenment, thus earning the status of an enlightened despot. As a patron of the arts she presided over the age of the Russian Enlightenment, a period when the Smolny Institute, the first state-financed higher education institution for women in Europe, was established.

First years

Catherine's father, Christian August, Prince of Anhalt-Zerbst, belonged to the ruling German family of Anhalt, but held the rank of a Prussian general in his capacity as Governor of the city of Stettin (now Szczecin, Poland). Born Sophia Augusta Fredericka (German: Sophie Friederike Auguste von Anhalt-Zerbst-Dornburg, nicknamed "Figchen") in Stettin, Pomerania, two of her first cousins became Kings of Sweden: Gustav III and Charles XIII. In accordance with the custom then prevailing in the ruling dynasties of Germany, she received her education chiefly from a French governess and from tutors. Catherine's childhood was quite uneventful. She once wrote to her correspondent Baron Grimm: "I see nothing of interest in it." Although Catherine was born a princess, her family had very little money. Catherine's rise to power was supported by her mother's wealthy relatives who were both wealthy nobles and royal relations.

The choice of Sophia as wife of her second cousin, the prospective tsar Peter of Holstein-Gottorp, resulted from some amount of diplomatic management in which Count Lestocq, Peter's aunt (the ruling Russian Empress Elizabeth), and Frederick II of Prussia took part. Lestocq and Frederick wanted to strengthen the friendship between Prussia and Russia to weaken Austria's influence and ruin the Russian chancellor Bestuzhev, on whom Empress Elizabeth relied, and who acted as a known partisan of Russo-Austrian co-operation. Catherine first met Peter III at the age of 10. Based on her writings, she found Peter detestable upon meeting him. She disliked his pale complexion and his fondness for alcohol at such a young age. Peter also still played with toy soldiers. Catherine later wrote that she stayed at one end of the castle, and Peter at the other.

The diplomatic intrigue failed, largely due to the intervention of Sophia's mother, Johanna Elisabeth of Holstein-Gottorp. Historical accounts portray her as a cold, abusive woman who loved gossip and court intrigues. Johanna's hunger for fame centred on her daughter's prospects of becoming empress of Russia, but she infuriated Empress Elizabeth, who eventually banned her from the country for spying for King Frederick of Prussia. The Empress Elizabeth knew the family well: she had intended to marry Princess Johanna's brother Charles Augustus (Karl August von Holstein), who had died of smallpox in 1727 before the wedding could take place. In spite of Johanna's interference, Empress Elizabeth took a strong liking to the daughter, who, on arrival in Russia in 1744, spared no effort to ingratiate herself not only with the Empress Elizabeth, but with her husband and with the Russian people. She applied herself to learning the Russian language with such zeal, she rose at night and walked about her bedroom barefoot, repeating her lessons (even though she mastered the language, she retained an accent). This led to a severe attack of pneumonia in March 1744. When she wrote her memoirs, she said she made up her mind when she came to Russia to do whatever was necessary, and to profess to believe whatever was required of her, to become qualified to wear the crown.

Princess Sophia's father, a devout German Lutheran, opposed his daughter's conversion to Eastern Orthodoxy. Despite his objection, on 28 June 1744 the Russian Orthodox Church received Princess Sophia as a member with the new name Catherine (Yekaterina or Ekaterina) and the (artificial) patronymic Алексеевна (Alekseyevna, daughter of Aleksey). On the following day, the formal betrothal took place. The long-planned dynastic marriage finally occurred on 21 August 1745 in Saint Petersburg. Sophia had turned 16; her father did not travel to Russia for the wedding. The bridegroom, known then as Peter von Holstein-Gottorp, had become Duke of Holstein-Gottorp (located in the north-west of present-day Germany near the border with Denmark) in 1739.

As she recalled in her memoirs, as soon as she arrived in Russia, she fell ill with a pleuritis that almost killed her. She credited her survival to frequent bloodletting; in a single day, she had four phlebotomies. Her mother, being opposed to this practice, fell into the Empress's disfavour. When her situation looked desperate, her mother wanted her confessed by a Lutheran priest. Awaking from her delirium, however, Catherine said: "I don't want any Lutheran; I want my orthodox father." This raised her in the Empress's esteem.

The newlyweds settled in the palace of Oranienbaum, which remained the residence of the "young court" for many years to come.

Count Andrei Shuvalov, chamberlain to Catherine, knew the diarist James Boswell well, and Boswell reports that Shuvalov shared private information regarding the monarch's intimate affairs. Some of these rumours included that Peter took a mistress (Elizabeth Vorontsova), while Catherine carried on liaisons with Sergei Saltykov, Grigory Grigoryevich Orlov (1734–1783), Alexander Vasilchikov, Grigory Potemkin, Stanisław August Poniatowski, and others. She became friends with Princess Ekaterina Vorontsova-Dashkova, the sister of her husband's mistress, who introduced her to several powerful political groups that opposed her husband. Peter III's temperament became quite unbearable for those who resided in the palace. He would announce trying drills in the morning to male servants, who later joined Catherine in her room to sing and dance until late hours. Catherine became pregnant with her second child, Anna, who only lived to four months, in 1759. Due to various rumours of Catherine's promiscuity, Peter was led to believe he was not the child's biological father and is known to have proclaimed, "Go to the devil!" when Catherine angrily dismissed his accusation. She thus spent much of this time alone in her own private boudoir to hide away from Peter's abrasive personality.

Reign of Peter III and the coup d'état of July 1762

After the death of the Empress Elizabeth on 5 January 1762, Peter succeeded to the throne as Emperor Peter III, and Catherine became empress consort. The imperial couple moved into the new Winter Palace in Saint Petersburg.

The tsar's eccentricities and policies, including a great admiration for the Prussian king, Frederick II, alienated the same groups that Catherine had cultivated. Besides, Peter intervened in a dispute between his Duchy of Holstein and Denmark over the province of Schleswig (see Count Johann Hartwig Ernst von Bernstorff).

Russia and Prussia fought each other during the Seven Years' War (1756–1763) until Peter's accession. Peter's insistence on supporting Frederick II of Prussia, who had seen Berlin occupied by Russian troops in 1760, but now suggested partitioning Polish territories with Russia, eroded much of his support among the nobility.

In July 1762, barely six months after becoming emperor, Peter took a holiday with his Holstein-born courtiers and relatives to Oranienbaum, leaving his wife in Saint Petersburg. On the night of 8 July (OS: 27 June 1762), Catherine the Great was given the news that one of her co-conspirators had been arrested by her estranged husband, and that all they had been planning must take place at once. She left the palace and departed for the Ismailovsky regiment, where she delivered a speech asking the soldiers to protect her from her husband. Catherine then left with the regiment to go to the Semenovsky Barracks, where the clergy were waiting to ordain her as the sole occupant of the Russian throne. She had her husband arrested, and forced him to sign a document of abdication, leaving no one to dispute her accession to the throne. On 17 July 1762—eight days after the coup and just six months after his accession to the throne—Peter III died at

Ropsha, at the hands of Alexei Orlov (younger brother to Grigory Orlov, then a court favourite and a participant in the coup). Historians find no evidence for Catherine's complicity in the supposed assassination.

At the time of Peter III's overthrow, other potential rival claimants to the throne existed: Ivan VI (1740–1764), in close confinement at Schlüsselburg, in Lake Ladoga, from the age of six months; and Yelizaveta Alekseyevna Tarakanova (1753–1775). Ivan VI was assassinated during an attempt to free him as part of a failed coup against Catherine: Catherine, like Empress Elizabeth before her, had given strict instructions that he was to be killed in the event of any such attempt. Ivan was thought to be insane because of his years of solitary confinement, so might have made a poor emperor, even as a figurehead.

Catherine, though not descended from any previous Russian emperor of the Romanov Dynasty (she descended from the Rurik Dynasty, which preceded the Romanovs), succeeded her husband as empress regnant. She followed the precedent established when Catherine I (born in the lower classes in the Swedish East Baltic territories) succeeded her husband Peter the Great in 1725.

Historians debate Catherine's technical status, some seeing her as a regent or as a usurper, tolerable only during the minority of her son, Grand Duke Paul. In the 1770s, a group of nobles connected with Paul (Nikita Panin and others) considered a new coup to depose Catherine and transfer the crown to Paul, whose power they envisaged restricting in a kind of constitutional monarchy. However, nothing came of this, and Catherine reigned until her death.

Coronation and Catherine Reign 1762

On 28 June 1762, with the aid of her lover Grigory Orlov, Catherine rallied the troops of Saint Petersburg to her support and declared herself Catherine II, the sovereign ruler of Russia, later naming her son Paul as her heir. She had Peter arrested and forced him to sign an act of abdication. When he sought permission to leave the country, she refused it, intending to hold him prisoner for life. He had only a few days to live, though, as shortly after his arrest, he was strangled to death by Catherine's supporters; though, no one knows what part Catherine had in Peter's death. She was crowned in Moscow on the 22 September 1762. Catherine's coronation marks the creation of one of the main treasures of the Romanov dynasty, the Imperial Crown of Russia, designed by Swiss-French court diamond jeweller Jérémie Pauzié. Inspired by the Byzantine Empire design, the crown was constructed of two gold and silver half spheres, representing the eastern and western Roman empires, divided by a foliate garland and fastened with a low hoop. The crown contains 75 pearls and 4,936 Indian diamonds forming laurel and oak leaves, the symbols of power and strength, and is surmounted by a 398.62-carat ruby spinel that previously belonged to the Empress Elizabeth, and a diamond cross. The crown was produced in a record two months and weighed only 2.3 kg. From 1762, the crown created by Jérémie Pauzié was the coronation crown of all Romanov emperors, till the monarchy's abolition and the death of last Romanov, Nikolas II, in 1918. It is one of the main treasures of the Romanov dynasty, and is now on display in the Moscow Kremlin Armoury Museum in Russia.

Russian Foreign affairs

During her reign, Catherine extended the borders of the Russian Empire southward and westward to absorb New Russia, Crimea, Northern Caucasus, Right-bank Ukraine, Belarus, Lithuania, and Courland at the expense, mainly, of two powers – the Ottoman Empire and the Polish–Lithuanian Commonwealth. All told, she added some 200,000 square miles (520,000 km²) to Russian territory.

Catherine's foreign minister, Nikita Panin (in office 1763–81), exercised considerable influence from the beginning of her reign. A shrewd statesman, Panin dedicated much effort and millions of rubles to setting up a "Northern Accord" between Russia, Prussia, Poland, and Sweden, to counter the power of the Bourbon–Habsburg League. When it became apparent that his plan could not succeed, Panin fell out of favour and Catherine had him replaced with Ivan Osterman (in office 1781–97).

Catherine agreed to a commercial treaty with Great Britain in 1766, but stopped short of a full military alliance. Although she could see the benefits of Britain's friendship, she was wary of Britain's increased power following its victory in the Seven Years War, which threatened the European balance of power.

Russo-Turkish Wars

While Peter the Great had succeeded only in gaining a toehold in the south on the edge of the Black Sea in the Azov campaigns, Catherine completed the conquest of the south. Catherine made Russia the dominant power in south-eastern Europe after her first Russo-Turkish War against the Ottoman Empire (1768–74), which saw some of the heaviest defeats in Turkish history, including the Battle of Chesma (5–7 July 1770) and the Battle of Kagul (21 July 1770).

The Russian victories allowed Catherine's government to obtain access to the Black Sea and to incorporate present-day southern Ukraine, where the Russians founded the new cities of Odessa, Nikolayev, Yekaterinoslav (literally: "the Glory of Catherine"; the future Dnepropetrovsk), and Kherson. The Treaty of Küçük Kaynarca, signed 10 July 1774, gave the Russians territories at Azov, Kerch, Yenikale, Kinburn, and the small strip of Black Sea coast between the rivers Dnieper and Bug. The treaty also removed restrictions on Russian naval or commercial traffic in the Azov Sea, granted to Russia the position of protector of Orthodox Christians in the Ottoman Empire, and made the Crimea a protectorate of Russia. Catherine annexed the Crimea in 1783, nine years after the Crimean Khanate had gained nominal independence—which had been guaranteed by Russia—from the Ottoman Empire as a result of her first war against the Turks. The palace of the Crimean khans passed into the hands of the Russians. In 1786, Catherine conducted a triumphal procession in the Crimea, which helped provoke the next Russo–Turkish War.

The Ottomans restarted hostilities in the second Russo-Turkish War (1787–92). This war, catastrophic for the Ottomans, ended with the Treaty of Jassy (1792), which legitimised the Russian claim to the Crimea and granted the Yedisan region to Russia.

Russo-Persian War

In accordance with the Treaty of Georgievsk (1783) Russia had signed with the Georgians to protect them against any new invasion of their Persian suzerains and further political aspirations, Catherine waged a new war against Persia in 1796 after they, under the new king Agha Mohammad Khan, had again invaded Georgia and established rule over it in 1795 and had expelled the newly established Russian garrisons in the Caucasus. The ultimate goal for the Russian government however was to topple the anti-Russian shah (king), and to replace him with a half-brother, namely Morteza Qoli Khan, who had defected to Russia, and was therefore pro-Russian.

It was widely expected that a 13,000-strong Russian corps would be led by a seasoned general (Gudovich)—but the Empress followed the advice of her lover, Prince Zubov, and entrusted the command to his youthful brother, Count Valerian Zubov. The Russian troops set out from Kizlyar in April 1796 and stormed the key fortress of Derbent on 10 May. The event was glorified by the court poet Derzhavin in his famous ode; he later commented bitterly on Zubov's inglorious return from the expedition in another remarkable poem.

By mid-June, Zubov's troops overran without any resistance most of the territory of modern-day Azerbaijan, including three principal cities — Baku, Shemakha, and Ganja. By November, they were stationed at the confluence of the Araks and Kura Rivers, poised to attack mainland Iran.

In that month, the Empress of Russia died and her successor Paul, who detested the Zubovs and had other plans for the army, ordered the troops to retreat to Russia. This reversal aroused the frustration and enmity of the powerful Zubovs and other officers who took part in the campaign: many of them would be among the conspirators who arranged Paul's murder five years later.

Relations with Western Europe

Catherine longed for recognition as an enlightened sovereign. She pioneered for Russia the role that Britain later played through most of the 19th and early 20th centuries as an international mediator in disputes that could, or did, lead to war. She acted as mediator in the War of the Bavarian Succession (1778–79) between the German states of Prussia and Austria. In 1780, she established a League of Armed Neutrality, designed to defend neutral shipping from the British Royal Navy during the American Revolution.

From 1788 to 1790, Russia fought a war against Sweden, a conflict instigated by Catherine's cousin, King Gustav III of Sweden, who expected to simply overtake the Russian armies still engaged in war against the Ottoman Turks, and hoped to strike Saint Petersburg directly. But Russia's Baltic Fleet checked the Royal Swedish navy in a tied battle of Hogland (July 1788), and the Swedish army failed to advance. Denmark declared war on Sweden in 1788 (the Theatre War). After the decisive defeat of the Russian fleet at the Battle of Svensksund in 1790, the parties signed the Treaty of Värälä (14 August 1790), returning all conquered territories to their respective owners and confirming the Treaty of Åbo. Peace ensued for 20 years, aided by the assassination of Gustav III in 1792.

Empress Catherine before the Mirror by Vigilius Eriksen-Bridgeman

Partitions of Poland

In 1764, Catherine placed Stanisław August Poniatowski, her former lover, on the Polish throne. Although the idea of partitioning Poland came from the King Frederick II of Prussia, Catherine took a leading role in carrying it out in the 1790s. In 1768, she formally became protector of the Polish–Lithuanian Commonwealth, which provoked an anti-Russian uprising in Poland, the Confederation of Bar (1768–72). After the uprising broke down due to internal politics in the Polish–Lithuanian Commonwealth, she established in the Rzeczpospolita, a system of government fully controlled by the Russian Empire through a Permanent Council, under the supervision of her ambassadors and envoys.

After the French Revolution of 1789, Catherine rejected many principles of the Enlightenment she had once viewed favourably. Afraid the May Constitution of Poland (1791) might lead to a resurgence in the power of the Polish–Lithuanian Commonwealth and the growing democratic movements inside the Commonwealth might become a threat to the European monarchies, Catherine decided to intervene in Poland. She provided support to a Polish antireform group known as the Targowica Confederation. After defeating Polish loyalist forces in the Polish–Russian War of 1792 and in the Kościuszko Uprising (1794), Russia completed the partitioning of Poland, dividing all of the remaining Commonwealth territory with Prussia and Austria (1795).

Last days of the Great Empress

Though Catherine's life and reign included remarkable personal successes, they ended with two failures. Her Swedish cousin (once removed), King Gustav IV Adolph, visited her in September 1796, the Empress's intention being that her granddaughter Alexandra should become Queen of Sweden by marriage. A ball was given at the imperial court on 11 September, when the engagement was supposed to be announced. Gustav Adolph felt pressured to accept the fact that Alexandra would not be converting to Lutheranism, and though he was delighted by the young lady, he refused to appear at the ball and left for Stockholm. Catherine was so irritated at this, her health was affected. She recovered well enough to begin to plan a ceremony where a favourite grandson would supersede her difficult son on the throne, but she died of a stroke before the announcement could be made, just over two months after the engagement ball.

On 16 November [O.S. 5 November] 1796, Catherine rose early in the morning and had her usual morning coffee, soon settling down to work on papers at her study. Her lady's maid, Maria Perekusikhina, had asked the Empress if she had slept well, and Catherine reportedly replied she had not slept so well in a long time. Sometime after 9:00 that morning, Catherine went to her dressing room and collapsed from a stroke while on the toilet. Worried by Catherine's absence, her attendant, Zakhar Zotov, opened the door and peered in. Catherine was sprawled on the floor. Her face appeared purplish, her pulse was weak, and her breathing was shallow and laboured. The servants lifted Catherine from the floor and brought her to the bedroom. Some 45 minutes later, the royal court's Scottish physician, Dr. John Rogerson, arrived and determined that Catherine had suffered a stroke. Despite all attempts to revive the Empress, she fell into a coma from which she never recovered. Catherine was given the last rites and died the following evening around 9:45. An autopsy performed on her body the next day confirmed the cause of death as stroke. (Later, several unfounded stories circulated regarding the cause and manner of her death.)

Catherine's undated will, discovered in early 1792 by her secretary Alexander Vasilievich Khrapovitsky among her papers, gave specific instructions should she die: "Lay out my corpse dressed in white, with a golden crown on my head, and on it inscribe my Christian name. Mourning dress is to be worn for six months, and no longer: the shorter the better." In the end, the empress was laid to rest with a gold crown on her head and clothed in a silver brocade dress. On 25 November, the coffin, richly decorated in gold fabric, was placed atop an elevated platform at the Grand Gallery's chamber of mourning, designed and decorated by Antonio Rinaldi. According to Elisabeth Vigée Le Brun: "The empress's body lay in state for six weeks in a large and magnificently decorated room in the castle, which was kept lit day and night. Catherine was stretched out on a ceremonial bed surrounded by the coats of arms of all the towns in Russia. Her face was left uncovered, and her fair hand rested on the bed. All the ladies, some of whom took turn to watch by the body, would go and kiss this hand, or at least appear to." A description of the Empress's funeral is written in Madame Vigée Le Brun's memoirs. Catherine was buried at the Peter and Paul Cathedral in Saint Petersburg.

FACTS ON THE LIFE AND REIGN OF CATHERINE THE GREAT

Catherine the Great's Lovers and Favorites

- Sergei Saltykov: 1753-1754
- Prince Stanislaw Poniatowski: 1756-1758
- Prince Grigory Orlov: 1759-1772
- Aleksandr Vasilchikov: 1772-1773
- Prince Grigory Potemkin: 1774-1776
- Pyotr Zavadovsky: 1776-1777
- Semyon Zorich: 1777-1778
- Ivan Rimsky-Korsakov: 1778-1779
- Aleksandr Lanskoy: 1780-1784
- Aleksandr Yermolov: 1785-1786
- Count Aleksandr Dmitriev-Mamonov: 1786-1789
- Prince Platon Zubov: 1789-1796

Chronology of the Lives of Catherine and Potemkin

- 1729 Sophia Augusta Fredericka of Anhalt-Zerbst (future Catherine the Great) is born in Stettin on the Baltic Sea
- 1739 Grigory Aleksandrovich Potemkin is born in the village of Chizhevo near Smolensk
- 1740 Frederick II (the Great) of Prussia and Maria Theresa of Austria ascend the throne
- 1741 Elizabeth Petrovna, daughter of Peter the Great, overthrows the infant Ivan VI and seizes the Russian throne
- 1744 Sophia arrives in Russia, converts to Russian Orthodoxy, becomes Grand Duchess Catherine, and is officially engaged to Grand Duke Peter
- 1745 Potemkin moves to Moscow and begins his studies
- 1745 Grand Duchess Catherine and Grand Duke Peter are married
- 1752 Catherine begins liaison with Sergei Saltykov
- 1754 Catherine gives birth to Paul Petrovich, the future Paul I (1796-1801)
- 1755 Potemkin is enrolled in the Horse Guards
- 1755 Catherine begins liaison with Stanislaw Poniatowski
- 1757 Potemkin visits St. Petersburg and is presented to Empress Elizabeth I in recognition of his academic success
- 1760 Potemkin is expelled from Moscow University for laziness
- 1760 George III of England ascends the throne
- 1761 Catherine begins affair with Grigory Orlov
- 1761 Potemkin leaves Moscow for St. Petersburg
- 1761 Empress Elizabeth I dies; Peter III ascends the throne
- 1762 Catherine gives birth to Aleksei Bobrinsky, her son by Grigory Orlov

·1762 Peter III is overthrown and murdered; Catherine is proclaimed empress

·1764 Stanislaw Poniatowski is elected king of Poland

·1765 Emperor Francis I dies; Joseph II of Austria becomes emperor and co-regent with his mother, Maria Theresa

·1767 Legislative Commission opens in Moscow; Potemkin serves as "Guardian of the Tatars and other Exotic Peoples"

·1768 First Russo-Turkish War (1768-74) begins

·1769 Potemkin volunteers for duty and leaves capital for the front

·1770 Potemkin awarded Orders of St. Anne and St. George for fighting at Fokshany, Brailov, and Giurgevo; Russian navy defeats Turks at Battle of Chesme

·1772 Gustav III of Sweden carries out coup to restore powers of the crown

·1772 First Partition of Poland

·1773 Grigory Orlov falls from grace; Aleksandr Vasilchikov becomes favorite

·1773 Pugachev Rebellion begins

·1774 Potemkin returns to capital; replaces Vasilchikov as favorite, and possibly marries Catherine

·1774 Louis XVI of France ascends the throne

·1774 Treaty of Kuchuk Kainardji ends First Russo-Turkish War

·1775 Pugachev is executed in Moscow

·1775 Zaporozhian Cossack Host destroyed; territory incorporated into Russian Empire

·1775 American War of Independence begins

·1776 Potemkin's favor ends; Pyotr Zavadovsky becomes favorite

·1776 American Declaration of Independence is signed

·1777 Semyon Zorich replaces Zavadovsky as favorite

·1777 Alexander Pavlovich, Catherine's grandson and the future Alexander I (1801-25), is born

·1778 Prussia declares war on Austria beginning War of the Bavarian Succession (1778-79)

·1780 Aleksandr Lanskoy becomes favorite

·1780 Catherine meets Joseph II in Mogilyov

·1780 Maria Theresa dies

·1781 Russo-Austrian treaty of alliance concluded

·1781 Battle of Yorktown ends land combat in American War of Independence

·1783 Russia annexes the Crimea; Treaty of Georgievsk makes Georgia a Russian protectorate

·1783 Potemkin is stricken with malaria; Grigory Orlov dies

·1783 Treaty of Versailles ends war of France and Spain with Great Britain

·1784 Treaty of Constantinople is signed by which Ottoman Porte recognizes annexation of Crimea

·1784 Potemkin officially founds city of Sevastopol

·1784 Favorite Aleksandr Lanskoy dies

·1785 Potemkin is appointed commander in chief of the Russian armed forces in case of war with the Porte

- 1785 Catherine issues charters to the nobility and towns
- 1786 Aleksandr Dmitriev-Mamonov becomes favorite
- 1786 Frederick the Great of Prussia dies; Frederick William II ascends the throne
- 1786 Potemkin founds Yekaterinoslav (Dnepropetrovsk)
- 1787 Catherine and Joseph II tour southern Russia and the Crimea with Potemkin
- 1787 The Porte declares war beginning Second Russo-Turkish War (1787-91)
- 1787 Drafting of U.S. Constitution
- 1788 Joseph II declares war on the Porte
- 1788 Triple Alliance among Britain, Prussia, and Holland is formed
- 1788 Gustav III attacks Russia beginning Russo-Swedish War (1788-90)
- 1788 Estates General are summoned in France
- 1788 Turkish fortress of Ochakov falls to Potemkin
- 1789 Sultan Abdul Hamid dies; succeeded by Selim III
- 1789 Fall of Mamonov; Platon Zubov becomes favorite
- 1789 Revolution begins in France; storming of the Bastille
- 1789 Russian victories over Turks at Fokshany, River Rymnik, Bender
- 1789 Russian naval victory over Swedes at First Battle of Svensksund
- 1789 Austrians take Belgrade and march into Bucharest
- 1789 George Washington is elected president of United States
- 1790 Alliance between Prussia and the Porte is signed
- 1790 Joseph II dies; Leopold II ascends the throne
- 1790 Defensive alliance signed by Prussia and Poland
- 1790 Convention of Reichenbach establishing armistice between Austria and the Porte is signed
- 1790 Treaty of Verela is signed ending Russo-Swedish War
- 1790 Russian victories over Turks at Tulcha and Ismail
- 1791 Ochakov Crisis: Britain and Prussia threaten Russia with war
- 1791 Potemkin visits St. Petersburg for last time
- 1791 Revolution in Poland: Constitution of 3 May
- 1791 Louis XVI flees Paris and is caught at Varennes
- 1791 Peace of Sistova is signed ending war between Austria and the Porte
- 1791 Potemkin dies on the way to Nikolaev
- 1791 Treaty of Jassy is signed ending Second Russo-Turkish War
- 1792 Gustav III is murdered in Sweden
- 1792 Russia invades Poland

·1792 Monarchy falls in France; France declares war on Austria

·1793 Louis XVI is executed in Paris; Reign of Terror begins

·1793 Second Partition of Poland

·1794 Polish insurrection is crushed by Russia

·1794 Robespierre is toppled in France

·1795 Third Partition of Poland

·1795 The Directory is put in power in France

·1796 Nicholas Pavlovich, Catherine's third grandson and the future Nicholas I (1825-55), is born

·1796 Catherine the Great dies; Paul I ascends the throne

Empress Catherine The Great 1787 (Mikhail Shibanov)

РИСУНКИ

ОДЕЖДЫ и ВООРУЖЕНІЯ

РОССІЙСКИХЪ

ВОЙСКЪ.

PLATES LIST OF ILLUSTRATIONS

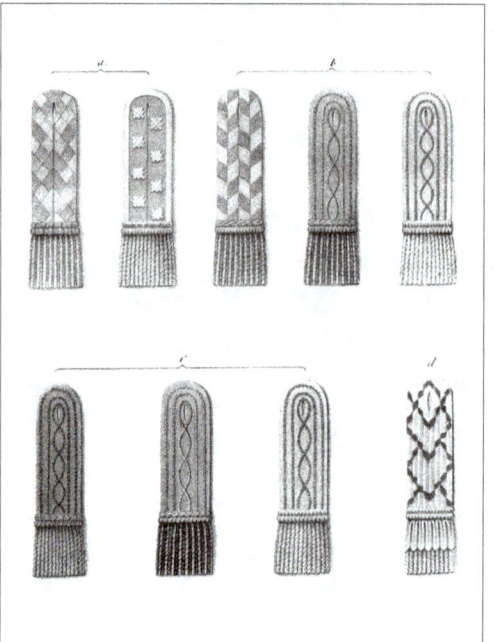

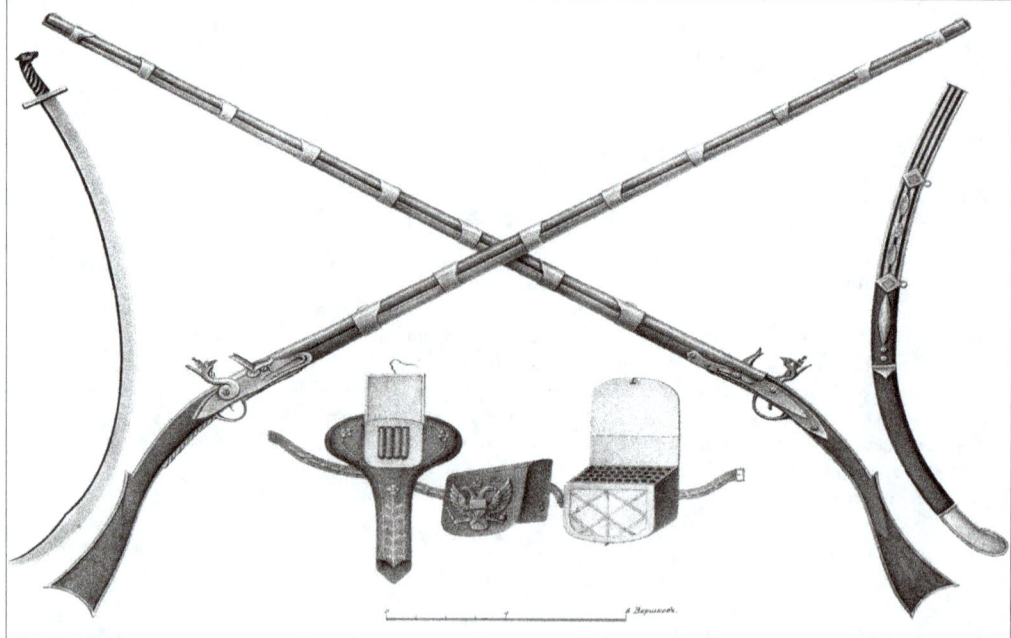

Pursuits of the Garrison Battalions, from 1764 to 1786 - Coat of arms of Garrison Battalions of the Dnieper line, approved on March 17, 1771 - Shotgun, Saber, Pistol Holster and Cartridge

Garrison Battalion, 1786-1796

Nonstroyovy Garrison Battalion, 1786-1796

Ober Officer of the Garrison Battalion from 1786 to 1796

Don Cossack of 1774

Volga Cossack of 1774

Don Cossack of 1774

Kizlyar and Astrakhan Cossacks of 1774

Mozdok Cossacks of 1774

Tobolsky Cossack of 1774

Chuguevsky Cossack Officer of 1774

Cossack Fortress of St. Demetrius, 1774

Azov and Taganrog Cossacks of 1774

Ekaterinoslav Kazak in 1788 and in 1789

Chuguevsky Cossack 1793-1796

Under Officer and Series of the 1ˢᵗ Battalion of the Greek Infantry Regiment, 1779-1796

Officer of the 1ˢᵗ Battalion of the Greek Infantry Regiment, 1779-1796

Under Officer, Serious and Officer of the 2nd Battalion of the Greek Infantry Regiment, 1779-1796

Musketeers of the Polish Corps: Sergeant and the 1794 Serf

821

Musketer of the Polish Corps in 1774

Grenader of the Polish Corps in 1774

Infantry Ober Officer of the Polish Corps in 1794

Infantry Hq Officer of the Polish Corps in 1794

Infantry Ober Officer of the Polish Corps in 1794

Native Polish Cavalry of the Polish Corps, 1794

Ober Officer of the People's Cavalry of the Polish Corps, 1794

Light Legged Regiment of the Polish Corps, 1794

Hq Officer of the Light-columned regiment of the Polish Corps in 1794

Hussar Regiment of the Ekaterinoslav Volunteers in 1787 and 1788

Gusar of the Convoy Squadrons of General-Field Marshal Prince Potemkin of Tavrichesky, 1788-1791

Serial Senate Battalion, 1787-1796

Officer of the Senate Battalion, 1787-1796

Branch of the Commissariat Company, 1764-1786

Officer of the Commissariat Company, 1764-1786

Musketer and the Grenader of Battalions from the House and Gardens Structure, 1765-1785

Series 'Workers' Company of Battalions from the Structure of Houses and Gardens, 1765-1785

Ober Officer of the Battalions from the House and Gardens Structure, 1765-1785

Private Provision Company, 1766-1786

Officer of the Provincial Company, 1766-1786

841

Private Provision Company, 1766-1786

Serious and Officer of the Team at the St. Petersburg Bank, 1793-1796

Serial Command at the Trinity Commercial Expedition, 1775-1796

Officer and the Serial Command at the College of Foreign Affairs, 1793-1796

Ranovye Gornozavodsky Battalion, 1764-1786

Gornozavod Officer 1764-1786

A Military Russian coat of arms

Serious and Officer of the Standing Teams: St. Petersburg Governorate, 1787-1796

Serious and Officers of the Established Commands: Riga, Vyborg and Revelsky Names, 1787-1796

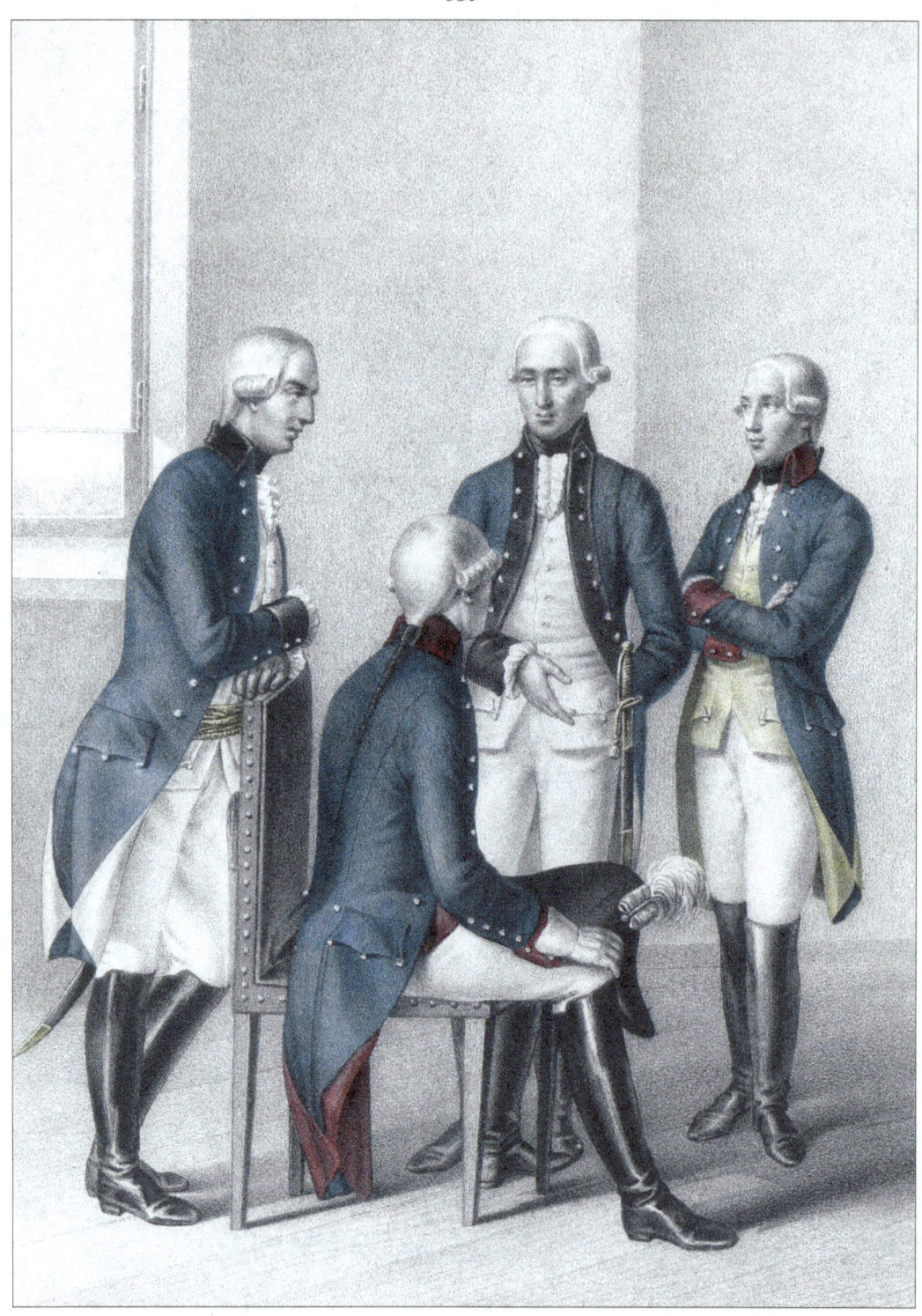

Officers of the Established Teams: Novgorod, Tver, Yaroslavl and Pskov Provinces, 1787-1796

Several Staff Commands: Vologda, Kostroma and Arkhangelsk Localities, 1787-1796

852

Officer of the fusilier regiment, from 1763 to 1786

Officers of the Established Teams: Moscow, Vladimir and Ryazan Provinces, 1787-1796

Serial Established Commands: Tambov, Tula, Kaluga and Orel Province, 1787-1796

Officers of the Established Teams: Kursk, Voronezh and Saratov Names, 1787-1796

Officers of the Established Teams: Penza, Kazan, Nizhny Novgorod, Simbirsk and Ufa Names, 1787-1796

Serial Commands: Irkutsk and Kolyvan Provinces, 1787-1796.

Officers of the Established Teams: Chernihiv, Kharkov and Novgorod-Seversky Localities, 1787-1796

Serious and Officers of the Established Teams: Polotsk, Smolensk and Magilev Provinces, 1787-1796

Officers of the Established Teams: the Taurida Region and the Chapters: Ekaterinoslav, Kiev and the Caucasus,

1787-1796

Serious and Officers of the Established Teams: Courland Province, in 1795 and 1796

Office of the Military Council 1764-1780

Pisec of the Military Collegium 1764-1786

General-Krig Kommisar 1764-1780

General Proviantmaster 1764-1780

Banners of the Grenadier and Infantry (Siberian) regiments. Approved on May 10, 1763.   Banner of the Infantry Regiment

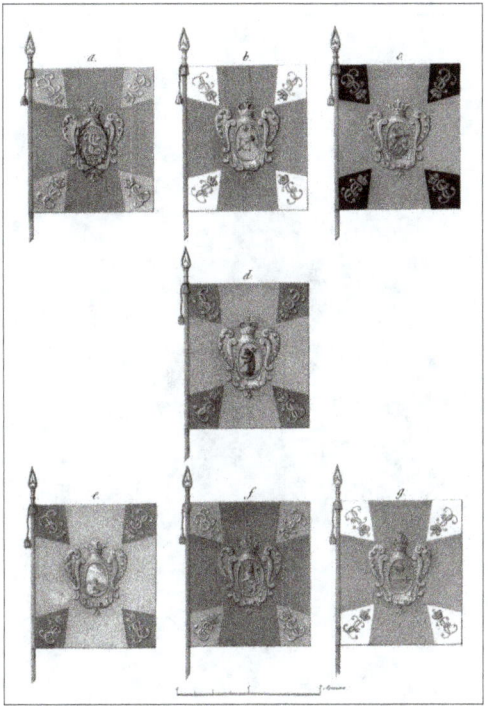

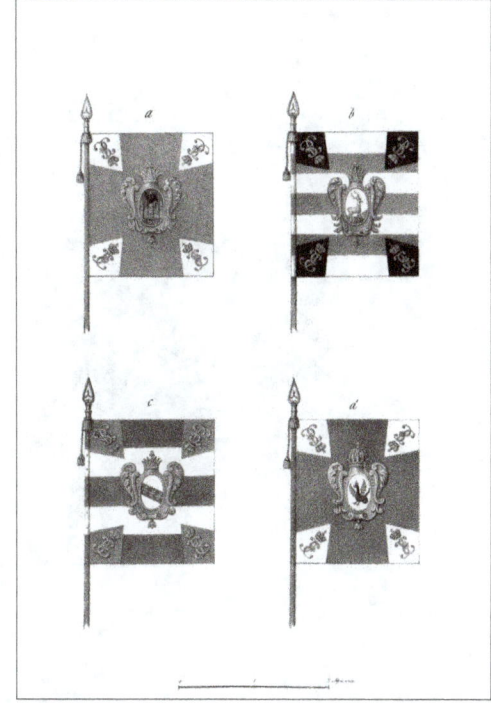

Banners of the infantry regiments, with division into divisions - Banner Light Field Command.   Approved on December 10, 1771

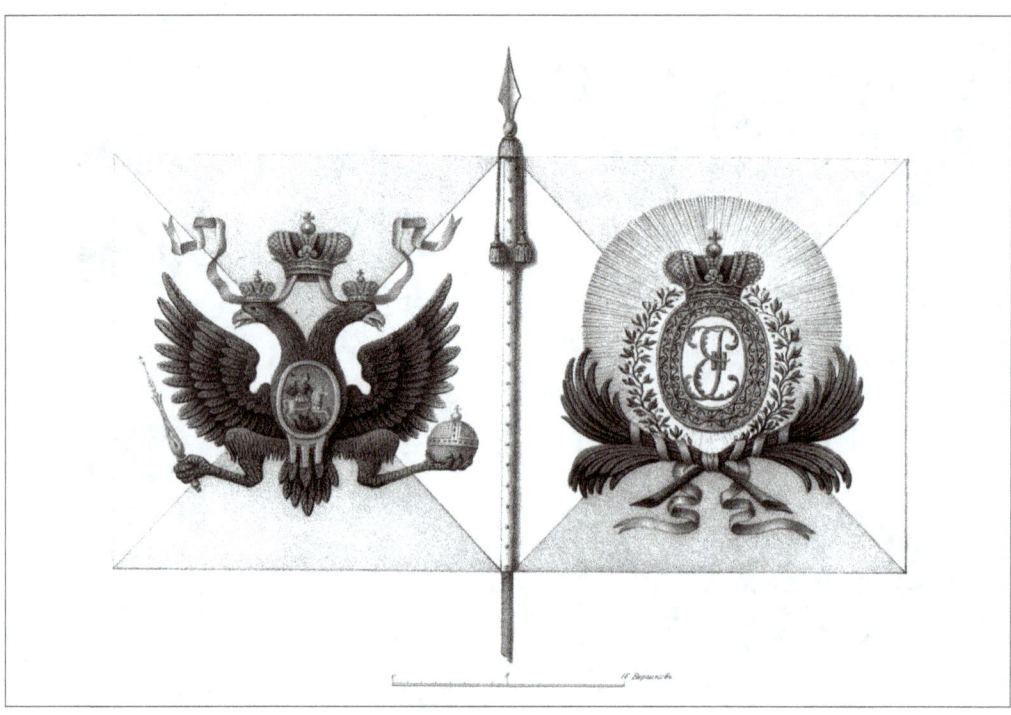

Banner of the Grenadier Regiment. Highest approved on November 11, 1780 · *Standards of the Cuirassier regiment*

Standard of the Kirassir Heir Regiment, 1778-1797

Standards of the Carabinier regiment (The

Ryazan Carabinieri), 1763-1780

Standards of the Carabinier regiment (Kargopolsky Carabinieri)

Banner of Bombardier Regiment, 1763-1796

Banners of the regiments of the L. Guard: Preobrazhensky, Semenovsky and Izmailovsky. Awarded in 1763 - Banner of the Land Cadet Corps - Banner of the Artillery and Engineer Cadet Corps, granted on June 23, 1785. Banner of the Corps of the Aliens of the Migrant People, granted on July 20, 1793

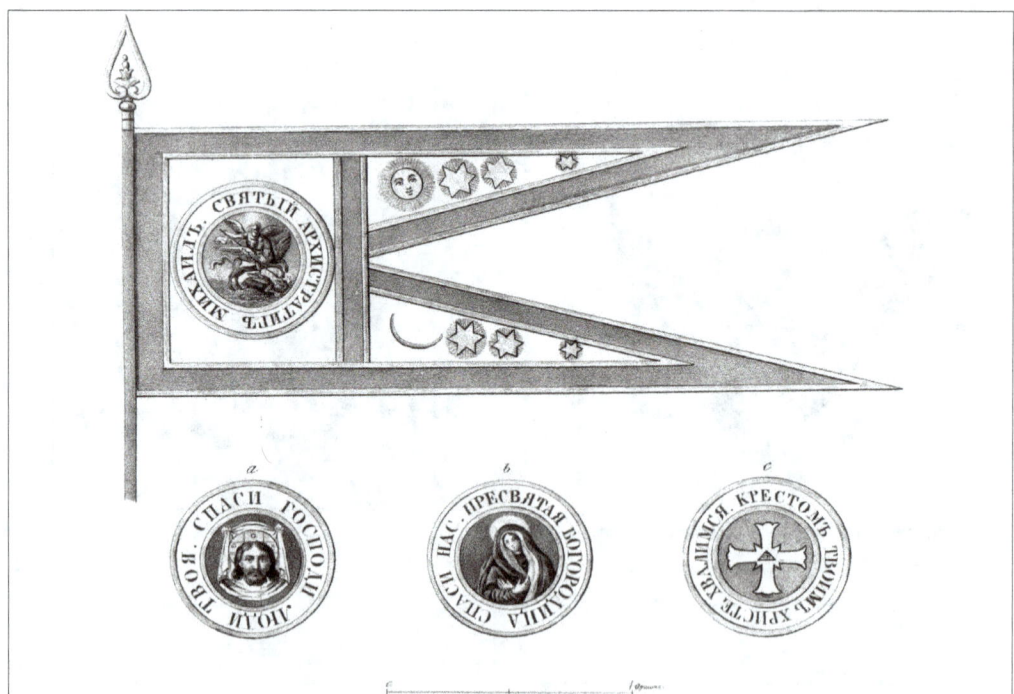

Banner of the Garrison (St. Petersburg) Battalion - Banner of the Don army, granted on July 9, 1764 The Terek Military Troops, granted in 1774

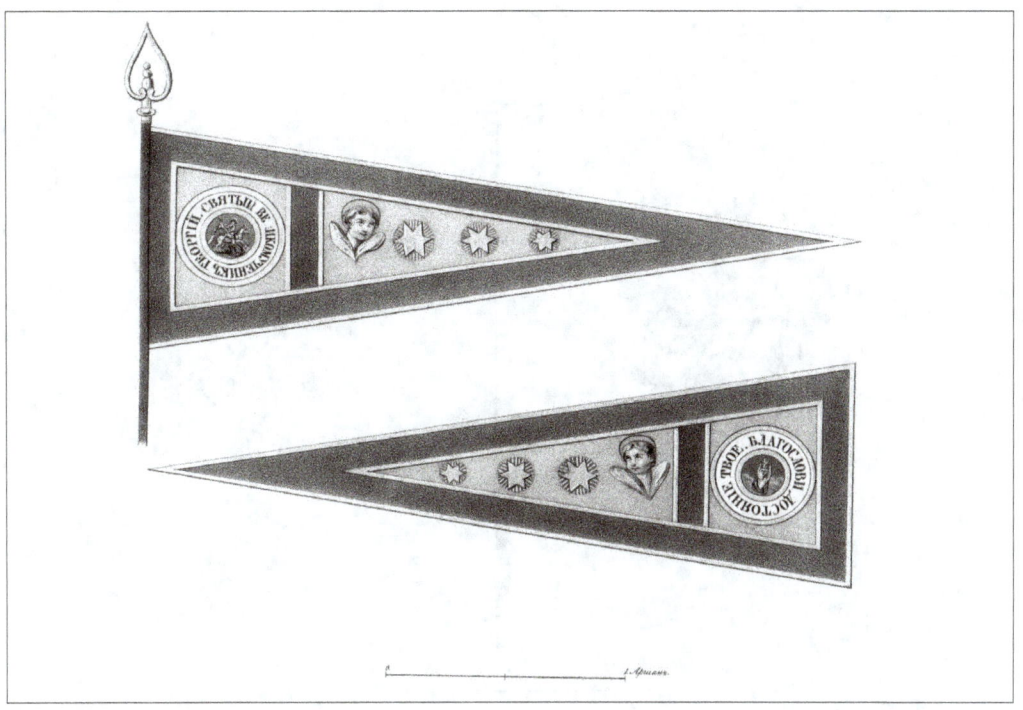

Grebensky Cossacks' Gorge, granted in 1774.

Banner of the Don Army, granted on December 9, 1776

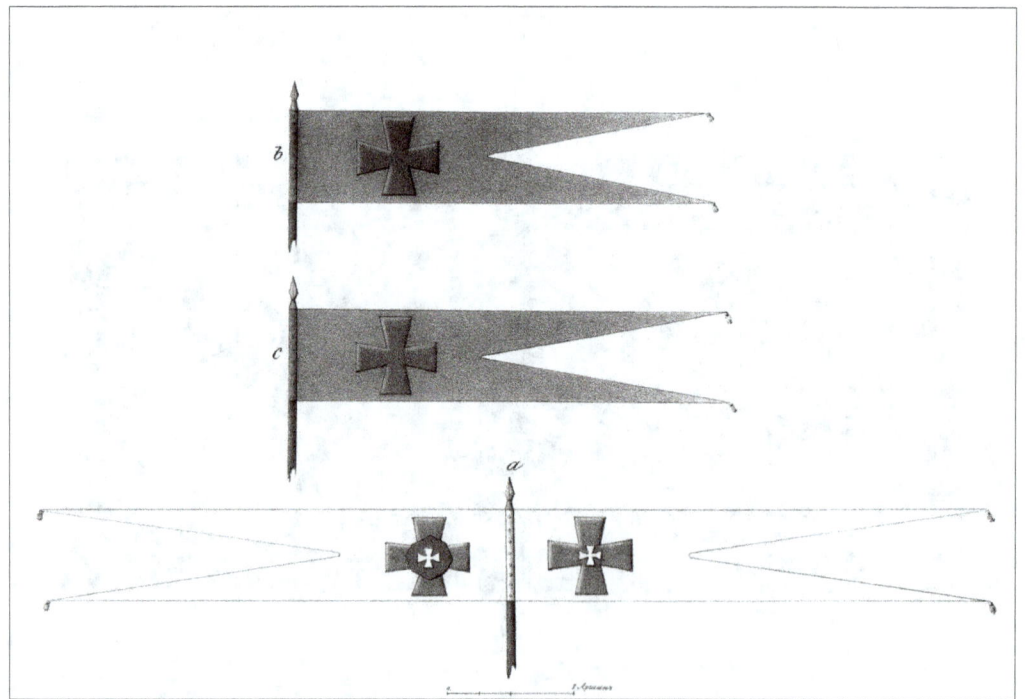

Flag and Banners of the Black Sea troops, granted on February 27, 1788

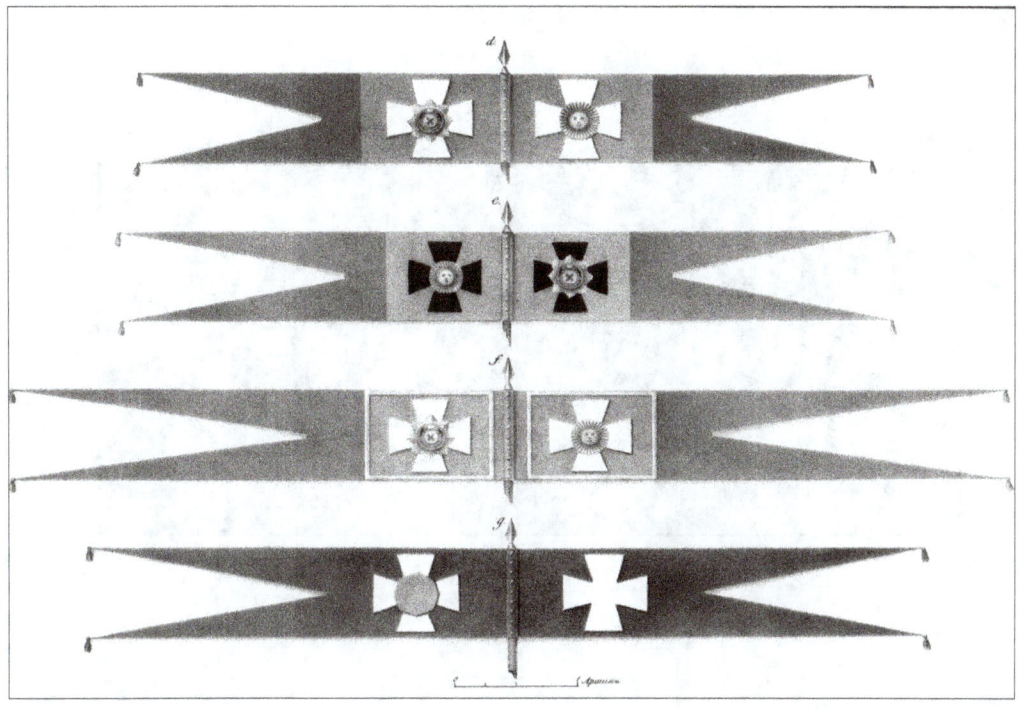

Banner of the Black Sea Troops and Flag of the Don army, granted in 1795

Banner an Russian decorations in 1769

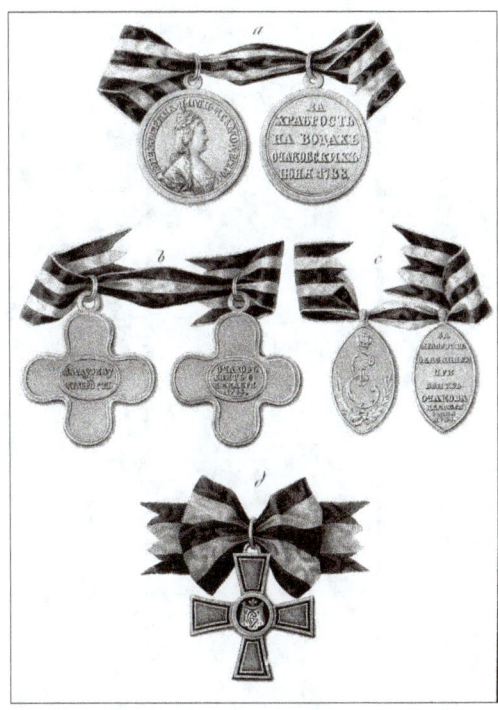

Russian decorations in 1770 to 1794

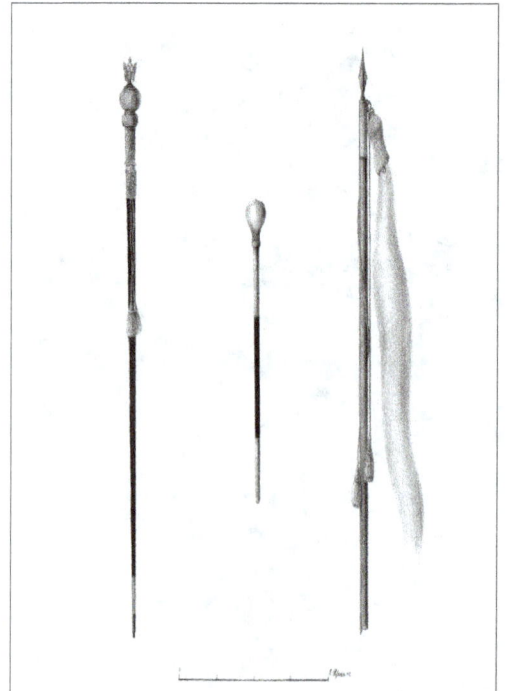

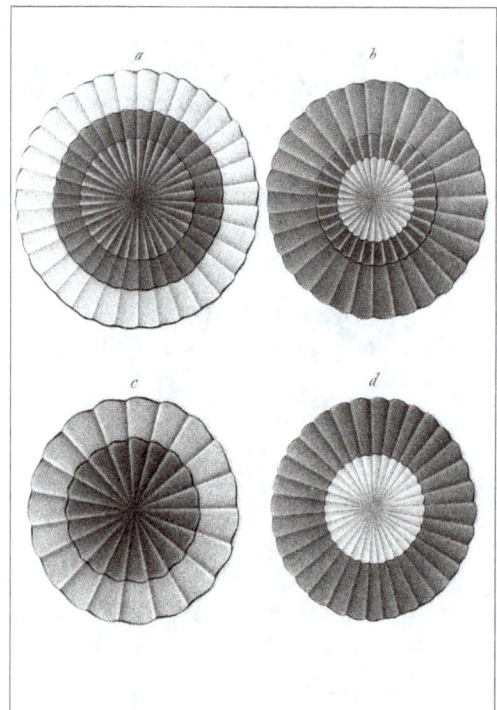
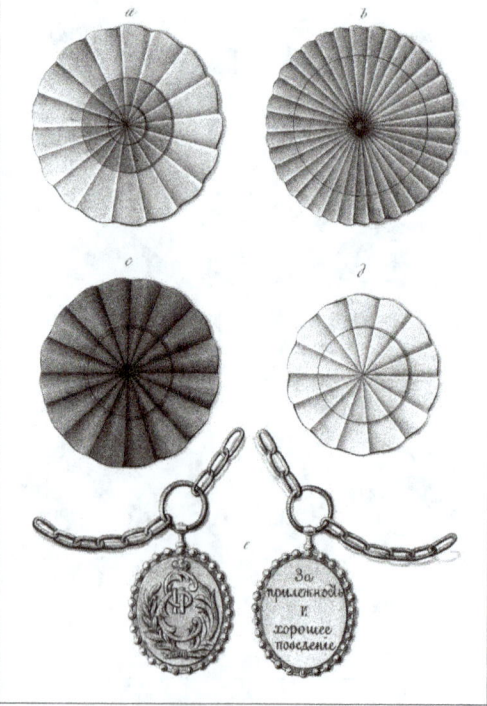

Medal signs for the Cadets of the 5th age of the Land Cadet Corps, from 1767 to 1796. Badges for the Cadets of the 3rd, 2nd and 1st ages of the Land Cadet Corps, from 1767 to 1796.

Musketer of the Gatchina troops of the Battalion of His Highness the Heir of 1793

Grenader and Musketer of the Battalions of the Gatchina troops: Major Ertel and Major Mertens in 1793

Grenaderskaya Shapka Gatchina troops Battalion Major Ortel

Eagle of the Gatchina troops 1793

Kirasir or the Gandard of the Gatchina troops 1793

Dragun Gatchina troops 1793

Gusar Gatchina troops 1793

Cossack of the Gatchina troops 1793

Pediment of the Artillery of the Gatchina troops in 1793

Riding Horse Artillery of the Gatchina troops of 1793

SOLDIERS, WEAPONS & UNIFORMS ALREADY PUBLISHED

(SOME TITLES)

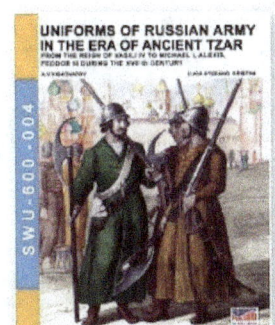

UNIFORMS OF RUSSIAN ARMY IN THE ERA OF ANCIENT TZAR
SWU-600-004

UNIFORMS OF RUSSIAN ARMY OF PETER I THE GREAT
SWU-700-006

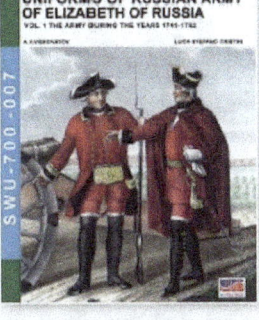

UNIFORMS OF RUSSIAN ARMY OF ELIZABETH OF RUSSIA
SWU-700-007

UNIFORMS OF RUSSIAN ARMY OF ELIZABETH OF RUSSIA
SWU-700-008

UNIFORMS OF RUSSIAN ARMY IN THE XVIII CENTURY VOL. 1
SWU-700-005

UNIFORMS OF RUSSIAN ARMY IN THE XVIII CENTURY VOL. 2
SWU-700-009

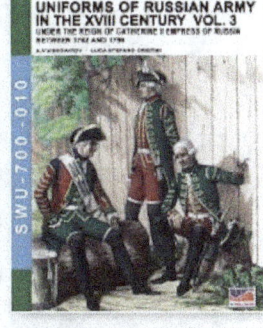

UNIFORMS OF RUSSIAN ARMY IN THE XVIII CENTURY VOL. 3
SWU-700-010

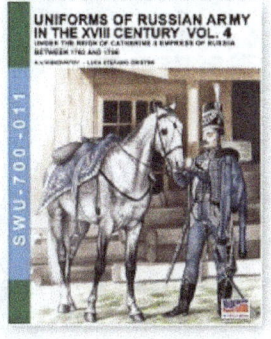

UNIFORMS OF RUSSIAN ARMY IN THE XVIII CENTURY VOL. 4
SWU-700-011

BRITISH ARMY UNIFORMS IN 1742
IN THE ART OF JOHN PINE
SWU-700-001

PRUSSIAN & AUSTRIAN ARMY UNIFORMS IN 1742-1770
SWU-700-002

THE FRENCH ARMY OF ANCIEN RÉGIME Volume 1
IN THE ART OF FELIX PHILIPPOTEAUX
SWU-700-003

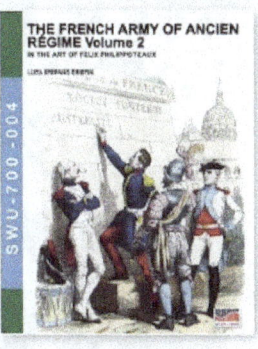

THE FRENCH ARMY OF ANCIEN RÉGIME Volume 2
IN THE ART OF FELIX PHILIPPOTEAUX
SWU-700-004

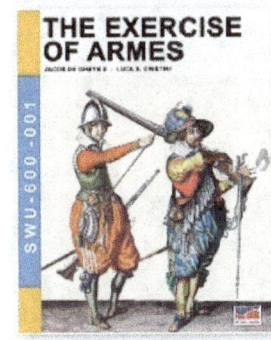

THE EXERCISE OF ARMES
SWU-600-001

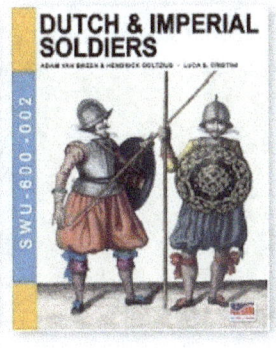

DUTCH & IMPERIAL SOLDIERS
SWU-600-002

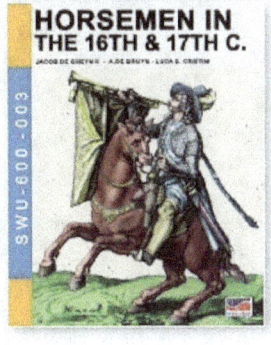

HORSEMEN IN THE 16TH & 17TH C.
SWU-600-003

IMPERIAL SOLDIERS & UNIFORMS 1640-1860
IN THE ART OF FRANZ GERASCH
SWU-GEN-001